OUT OF THE
DRAWING ROOM—
AND INTO THE ARENA!

When Bruce Becker first learned backgammon, he learned it the easy way, the Drawing Room way— and, like plenty of other beginning players, he soon got bored with the game. But one lucky day, he happened upon a full-tilt, damn-the-torpedoes backgammon game played by two guys who were out for blood. And that's when Bruce Becker learned what backgammon was *really* all about!

Now he's written it all down—the rules, the strategies, the unparalleled *excitement* of backgammon— in the one backgammon book that gives you both the playing tools and the "psyching" skills you need to win—and win big!

BACKGAMMON
for BLOOD

**BRUCE
BECKER**

AVON
PUBLISHERS OF BARD, CAMELOT AND DISCUS BOOKS

AVON BOOKS
A division of
The Hearst Corporation
959 Eighth Avenue
New York, New York 10019

Backgammon Board designed by Charlotte and Steve Gellar
for Sybarite Ltd., N.Y.C., N.Y., courtesy of The Gammon Shop.
Photo by Norman Snyder

First Avon Printing, July, 1975
Sixth Printing

AVON TRADEMARK REG. U.S. PAT. OFF. AND
FOREIGN COUNTRIES, REGISTERED TRADEMARK—
MARCA REGISTRADA, HECHO EN CHICAGO, U.S.A.

Printed in the U.S.A.

For Bobbi,
who began it all,
and
For Sara,
for whom it was worthwhile

Friends always help in the preparation of a book; I'd like to express my appreciation to a few of mine:

Gail Frank
Joseph Bailey
Roberta Kent
Milton Witchel
Dr. Robert Bross
Michael Halberian
Richard Seaver
Ron and Isobel Konecky

CONTENTS

BACKGAMMON for BLOOD

1. SCIENCE AND CHANCE, AND THE SCIENCE OF CHANCE

When I was first learning the game of backgammon, I bought a copy of one of the few books then on the market, which I was told would give me the basic rules and an idea of the opening moves. It was true: the book explained these, but that was *all* it did. I learned the rules, played a few games, and quickly lost interest, just as I had years before in checkers. Quite frankly, I could not understand any of the feelings of excitement I had been told existed for the game.

One evening a few weeks later I went into Knickers, a pub I frequent, for dinner. From one of the booths I heard dice rolling, and so I stopped to investigate. There, playing backgammon, were the owner and a friend, and they were playing the game I thought I had learned. But in fact my

game bore very little resemblance to the one they were playing. Their dice were continually spinning, the checkers
moved faster than I could comprehend the moves, the
doubling cube—an indispensable aid to nail-biting games,
and which I had read a definition of but didn't understand—
kept increasing in amount. The excitement, even of the
spectators, was like that I had experienced at the craps table
in Vegas or the roulette wheel in Monte Carlo. It just was
not the same game I had learned. Now there was a vitality,
an excitement, a life to the game and the players that per-
meated the air. I suddenly realized that I was watching not
merely a game for sport, but a gladiators' contest, in the full
sense of the word: these men were going for the jugular; they
were playing for blood!

For five hours I stood there, entranced. I forgot dinner.
I forgot to walk my dog. I forgot sleep. I was hooked.

I have since learned the game the real way—the way it
has intrigued and excited and thrilled players for thousands
of years. And now that I can play the game the only way
it should be played, now that I know five-hour sessions of
enchantment are the rule and not the rarity, now that I
know there is always a winner and a tie is impossible, I am
even more hooked.

And that's what I want you to be, too—hooked—which is
why I have written this book to help you to play backgammon in the same fashion—that is, for blood.

That attitude is how this book differs from any other
written on backgammon today. I am not concerned with the
"sport" of the game, for any game is, of course, a sport in
that sense. I am concerned with making backgammon that
much more fun for you if, in addition to the sport of it, I can
help you to win; it is perfectly obvious that the fun of playing is not as great as the fun of playing *and winning*. And,
whether the stakes are money (in my opinion, they should

always be) or the admiration of the spectators (and, in particular, a particular one), winning is always the better way to play.

A lot has been written about the luck of backgammon, mostly having to do with the fact that dice are used to determine the play. Much has also been written about the luck of dice and what can, should, or can't be done about it. However, nothing about the luck of the dice has been written by the only consistent winners at dice—the casino owners. The reason is simple: they know there is no such thing. To these people, for whom the craps tables are the cornerstones of their gambling empires, the "luck" of the dice is meaningless, for they know that luck is for losers. This is because they depend completely and solely on a science: the science of probability. This is what consistently determines winners at dice, or in games based upon dice—not luck. Do you want proof? Have you ever heard of a casino operator going bust?

In a short burst of play, of course, luck can be meaningful. There is no question but that a fairly good player can often beat a so-called expert; we have all seen those games where a bad move is suddenly converted by what would otherwise be a poor throw into a stroke of genius. And, sometimes, when his dice are running hot, game after game can be won by the lesser player. There are days when you shouldn't have gotten out of bed, and there are others when you can do no wrong. But over a period of time (for once you know backgammon, you will play frequently), the luck will average out, and the laws of probability will take over, with this mathematical science inexorably governing the net results. However, I even have some tips to help you through those periods when luck seems to be going away from you, and help you take advantage of it when it's with you. Nor do you have to be a mathematical genius to understand or apply any of this science—you can utilize it fully if you can count up to 36!

Further, there are two advantages in the application of the laws of probability that you have in backgammon which do not exist in craps, both of which help you considerably. For one, in craps the player has to declare himself *before* he throws the dice. He makes his bet, then waits for the laws of probability to wipe him out. In backgammon, the reverse is true. The player throws his dice, and after studying his position, planning his strategy, and anticipating the probabilities his next throw involves, then makes his move. This leads to the second important difference, which is of the essence in the practical strategy of the game: before making his move, the player can utilize the same laws of probability to anticipate his opponent's next throw of the dice, enabling him to make his most advantageous move with this knowledge in mind!

It is these laws of probability, and their specific application to the game of backgammon, that this book presents, so that you will always know what strategic moves to make, and why; so that you will not need to depend on the fickle and ephemeral luck; so that you too can play backgammon for blood—*and win*.

If you are a beginner, relax: backgammon is not a difficult game to learn. On the contrary, it is extremely simple. But its simplicity is deceptive, and in fact it is the complexity of the contest after you learn the rules of playing that makes it so continually fascinating. For example, the rules for moving men couldn't be simpler, yet in the first two moves of the game—the opening and the response—over 100,000 combinations of moves are possible! This is a true figure, almost incredible in its scope, and fun to know—but thoroughly useless. In practice, there are 21 combinations of the dice that govern your move. I will give you what I think are the best openers for each and tell you why I have chosen them, based on the laws of probability and the strategy I advocate. As for the responses, if I am to suggest only the preferred response of each throw to each opener, I would have to give you 441 separate responses—a task beyond both this book and your desire. Instead, I will give you the principles of probability that will help you make the best response, as well as some specific and pertinent hints.

You can see that, with this kind of complexity in the opening two moves alone, backgammon can be continually exciting in its changes and challenges; and you can also see why you will need all the help you can get.

To get the most out of this book, I urge you to take out your set and arrange the moves as they are described. This will help fix some of the principles in your mind on the visual level. It may help even more if you work with a partner in plotting out some of the intricacies; it is surprising how much a discussion will add to your knowledge. The notation system I use to describe moves is simple: the points on your opponent's board are called B1 through B12, and the points on your board W1 through W12.

Finally, you will not become a great backgammon player simply by reading this book. You will have to play and play and play, learning, applying, and possibly adapting the principles I recommend here. I have found, however, that the best motivation to help you become a good player is to play for money. There is nothing like losing a few dollars because of a stupid mistake to keep you from ever making it again.

Happy blood-letting!

2. BASICS FOR BEGINNERS

Backgammon is a very easy game to learn; its very simplicity is, paradoxically, one of the main reasons for its relative lack of broad-based popularity over the years. Most people know it as "the game with all the points on the back of the checkerboard." The instructions on how to play accompanying these boards are equally simplistic—if you can understand them at all. Thus, if one is so inclined, or possibly merely inquisitive, the board may be set up and a game played out once or twice, with total boredom as the (predictable) result. The standard reaction is, "Well, I've tried it, and it just didn't turn me on." Unfortunately, this is not only true but understandable. Nothing in the way the game is described in those four-page (at most) instruction sheets would turn anyone on, and if I read one of them today it might even turn me off.

This said, I must admit that the instructions here are equally simplistic, but, hopefully, more understandable. However, they are accompanied by an admonition—have faith, this is just the beginning. After you learn these few rules, we'll get into the fun and excitement of the game.

To play, here's what you need:

(1) Two players.
(2) A board.
(3) Thirty checkers or men; fifteen of them in one color and fifteen in another.
(4) Two dice.

Let's discuss each element.

THE PLAYERS

Backgammon is played by two players, although in a variation of the game called chouette (on which there is a separate chapter) more can participate. However, they act only as advisers and bettors; therefore the game in essence is a two-person affair. Throughout this book, you will be called White, and your opponent Black.

THE BOARD

The game is played on a board; almost everyone has a vague idea of what the board looks like because it's on the back of most checkerboards that can be bought in any ten-cent store. The same game can also be played on a board from one of the luxury leather goods houses, costing hundreds of dollars. Either way, it's the same game; it's merely the aesthetics that change. I have one comment about the board, however: be sure to play on at least a decent-sized one, for you will find a small board very uncomfortable and tiring. I find that the medium-sized board (about 14 by 16 inches, opened) is as small as one should go; it also has the advantage of being the right size for the fold-down tables in airplanes.

This is what a board looks like:

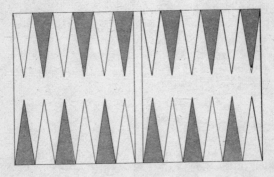

DIAGRAM 1

There are several things to note. There are twenty-four points on the board, twelve on each side. Although they are triangularly shaped and alternately colored, neither the shape nor the colors are of importance. Some manufacturers like red and white, others green and white. Louis Vuitton (surprisingly) doesn't make boards in his own brown and yellow; he uses black and yellow. The points are used in counting the moves and can just as readily be straight lines; the alternating colors simply make it easier and faster to count. Some wooden boards from Greece and the Mid-east don't have colored points; they are a bore to count on, and mistakes are more frequent.

The board is thought of as being divided into four quarters, which are sometimes called tables. However, in most places these sections themselves are also called boards, and I shall do so here. These four quarters are called your inner board, your outer board, your opponent's inner board, and your opponent's outer board. As you face your opponent, you can play with the inner board on your right or on your left. Which way is immaterial; one is merely the mirror image of the other. (This positioning of the board derives from the fact that in olden days the table was set up so that the inner board was always nearer to the source of light.) For the illustrations in this book, I shall use the inner board on the right, as in Diagram 2.

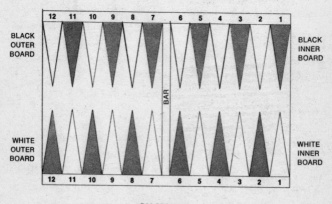

DIAGRAM 2

However, you can see that Black has to play with the inner board to his left; ultimately, therefore, it will be necessary for you to play either way, since in every game one player has the inner board on his right and one player has it on his left. (It would be a little ridiculous if you had to try to find only "left-handed" players!) Don't fret about this, and learn it the one way for now; once you watch a few games and play yourself you will find that you are not even conscious of this difference.

There are six points on each of the two inner boards and each of the two outer boards; the inner boards are separated from the outer boards by what is called the "bar." Starting on the inner board, the points are numbered 1 through 12 for you and the same for your opponent. These numbers and the designations of "inner" and "outer" boards are never printed on the board; you have to retain them in your mind. In describing moves, I will use as a notation system the designations B1, B2, B3, etc., for the points on Black's side of the board and W1, W2, W3, etc., for the points on your side of the board. The 7 point is sometimes called the "bar point" and the inner board the "home board"; you should know these terms in case you play in a fancy club.

THE MEN

Each player has fifteen men; here too the colors are immaterial and are necessary only to distinguish your men from your opponent's. To start the game, they are set up a shown in Diagram 3:

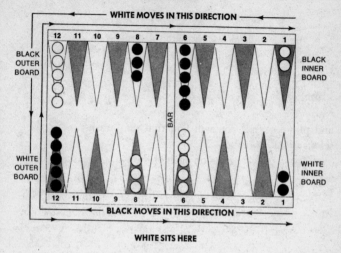

BLACK SITS HERE

WHITE MOVES IN THIS DIRECTION

BLACK OUTER BOARD

BLACK INNER BOARD

BAR

WHITE OUTER BOARD

WHITE INNER BOARD

BLACK MOVES IN THIS DIRECTION

WHITE SITS HERE

DIAGRAM 3

THE OBJECTIVE

To win, you must get all of your men off the board before your opponent does. To do this, you must move your men around the board in the direction shown in Diagram 3, from your opponent's inner board, to his outer board, to your outer board, and then in to your inner board. You must get all of your men into your inner board before you can begin to take them off the board, a process called "bearing off." Your opponent, of course, is trying to do the same, in the opposite direction.

TO BEGIN

Usually the matter of choice of colors and direction of play is amicably resolved; if there is a question, you should avoid premature bloodshed by the toss of the dice. The game is begun by each player throwing a single die. The one who gets the higher number makes the opening move; the first move is determined by these two dice: his own die, and his opponent's. Thereafter, the players alternate turns; each player throws both of his own dice and moves accordingly.

THE MOVES

The moves are always dictated by the throw of the dice. You must move any one man the number of points indicated by one die (starting to count from the point adjacent to the one you are moving from), and then either the same man or another man (as you wish) the number of points indicated on the other die. Learn to count the moves individually for each die: that is, don't add them together, as this is amateurish and can sometimes mislead you. For example, a 6 and 5 on the dice can be played as a six move and a five move, or as a five move and a six move; it is not an eleven move.

In moving, you pass over and count every point, whether there are men on it or not. But you must be able to end each move on a point that is either open and has no men on it, or has your own men on it, or has only *one* of your opponent's men on it. If the point has two or more of his men on it, then it is called "covered," "blocked," or "a closed door," and you are not allowed to land on it. However, you can pass over it when making your move, and you must count it while doing so. There is no limit to the number of men of one color that may be on a point.

If a point has only one man on it, that man is called a "blot," and he is "hit" if he is landed on by the opponent. It is not necessary to hit a blot; that is, you are not required to land on a blot if you have another possible move. Being hit puts this man on the bar; any man on the bar has to start from the beginning, a process called "entering," which we'll come to after this illustration.

Assume Black won the opening by throwing a 4 while you threw a 3. Of the various moves he can make, let's assume that he moves one man from the W1 to the W5 point (four points) and one man from the W12 to the B10 (three points). The board then looks like this:

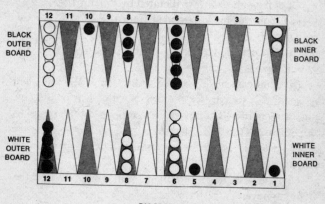

DIAGRAM 4

It is your turn and you throw a 5 - 4. You can move one of your men on B1 to B5 (four points) and then the same man from B5 to B10 (five points) where you hit the Black blot and send it to the bar. Note that the move could not be made by counting the 5 die first, as this would have moved your man from B1 to B6, and he is not allowed to land on this point because Black has at least two men covering it. This is an important principle; there are many times when a move is prevented because several intervening points are covered, even though the point you would like to land on by totaling your dice is open.

Let's assume in this same diagram that you throw a 5 - 2. You have these alternatives:

(1) You can move one man from the B1 to the B3 point, but that's all; you cannot make the five point move from there because the B8 point is covered. Nor can you move from B1 to B6 for the five points, because B6 is also covered by your opponent.

(2) You can move one man from B12 to W11 for the two-point move.

(3 You can move one man from B12 to W8 for the five-point move.

(4) You can move one man from B12 to W8 and then the same man to W6, for the full move of five points and then two points. (This move can also be made by going from B12 to W11 and then to W6).

(5) You can move one man from W8 to W6 for the two-point move.

(6) You can move one man from W8 to W3 for the five-point move.

(7) You can move one man from W8 to W3 and then the same man to W1, for the full move of five points and two points. This, of course, also hits the Black blot on W1 and puts him on the bar.

(8) You can move one man from W6 to W4, for the two-point move.

(9) You can move one man from W6 to W1, for the five-point move, here too hitting the Black blot on W1.

You should understand that these alternatives can be used any way you wish, as long as you make an allowable move for each die. For example, you might decide to play this throw by moving one man from B12 to W11 and one man from W6 to W1. Or you might decide to move one man from B12 to W11 and one man from B12 to W8. The way you choose among these possibilities and play your men has to do with the strategy of the game, which is what the rest of this book is about.

If you throw a double—that is, if both dice show the same number—then you must move that number of points four times. You can do this with any of five possible combinations of men, provided only that the points are not covered by your opponent. For example, if you throw a double 3, you can move:

(1) any one man four consecutive moves of three points each;

(2) any two men, each for two consecutive moves of three points per move;

(3) any one man three points, and any other man three consecutive moves of three points each;

(4) any two men three points each, and any other man two consecutive moves of three points each;

(5) any four men three points each.

There are two rules concerning moves you should be aware of: the first is that you *cannot* refuse to make your move if one is possible. The second is that if it is possible for you to make one move *or* the other, but not both, then you must make the move shown by the higher of the two dice.

ENTERING A MAN FROM THE BAR

When you have a man (or men) on the bar, you cannot make any other move until he (or they) gets back on the board. To do so, you must throw a number on either die that corresponds to a point in your opponent's inner board that is not covered by him. You can come in on this point, and then you must move that man or any other man the number of points shown on the other die. If he should have a blot on the point you come in on, you may hit it as well.

Let's assume the situation in Diagram 5:

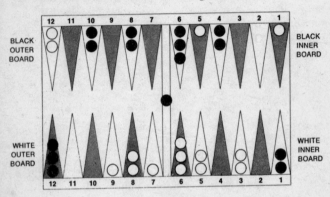

DIAGRAM 5

Here Black has been hit and is on the bar. He can enter if he throws a 1 (on his own point) or a 2 or 4; he cannot come in if he throws a 3 - 5, 3 - 6, 5 - 6, 3 - 3, 5 - 5, or 6 - 6. And until he comes in, he is not allowed to make any other move; in effect, he has lost his turn.

Let's assume that he throws a 5 - 2. He cannot come in on the W5 point because it is covered by you, but he can come in on the W2 point. He then can hit your blot on the W7 point with this W2 man for his 5 move. He can also let this man remain on the W2 and instead hit your blot on the B5 point from his B10 point, hoping to both delay you and possibly get your other blots on a later throw.

If you have two or more men on the bar, you must get them all in before you can make any other move. It may be that you can enter only one man on that first throw and will have to wait for your next turn to try to get the second man in. If your opponent has covered several points in his inner board, having a man on the bar can materially—perhaps vitally—slow you down.

MAKING POINTS

You can see that when you have hit your opponent's blot, he can lose a turn or more if he cannot easily enter your inner board. Therefore the more points you have covered in it, the harder it becomes for him to come in; consequently, there is a certain value in covering these points. However, there are other aspects to the strategy of the game; in other chapters I will get into the question of battle tactics such as why covering inner board points too early is not wise.

For the moment, you should become familiar with making points and learning how to count quickly to do this. Certain throws are obvious, and you will get to know them quickly. For example, if you have a 6 - 1 throw, an obvious move is to make the W7 point by moving one man from B12 and one man from W8, as illustrated in Diagram 6 on page 18.

Or, if you throw a 3 - 1, the move is to make the W5 point by moving one man from W8 to W5 and one man from W6 to W5.

In each case, you used what are called "builders"—that is, men who are not necessary to cover a point, and so can be moved to another point to build it. Builders can also mean blots, since blots can be built on or moved, depending on the throw of the dice.

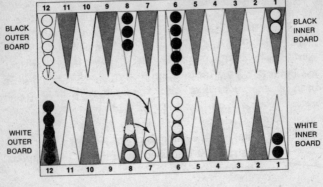

DIAGRAM 6

If you manage to cover all six points in your inner board by having two or more men on each of these points, you have what is known as a "prime." Should your opponent have a man on the bar, then he need not even pick up the dice, since he can throw only a 1 through 6 and all of these points are closed against him. He has to sit and wait until you open up one of these points before he can even try to come in. If you have covered any other six consecutive points—for example, the 4, 5, 6, 7, 8, and 9 points—it is called a "side prime," and should your opponent have a man on your 1, 2, or 3 points, he is locked in there until you open up one of your covered points, since he cannot throw anything larger than a 6 and so cannot move this man.

BEARING OFF

Once you have brought all your men around the board and into your inner board, you are ready to bear off: that is, to remove your men from the board. Once borne off, the man is then out of the game, and the first player to get all his men off the board wins.

You cannot bear off unless and until *all* your men are in your inner board. Therefore, if you should leave a blot that your opponent hits, this man must re-enter the board and get back into your inner board before you are allowed to bear off any more men, even if you have already taken some of your men off. This tactic of your opponent's, keeping some of his men in your inner board in an attempt to hit you at this latter stage of the game, is called a "back game," and is one of the strategies discussed in detail in the chapters dealing with tactics.

You bear off according to the dice. For each die thrown, you may remove a man from the point which corresponds to the number thrown, or you may instead move a man within the board the proper number of points. For example, if you throw a 6 - 3, you may remove one man from your 6 point and one man from your 3 point. But suppose your opponent still has two men on your 1 point, waiting hopefully to get a shot at a blot you have to leave, and you only have two men on the 6 point:

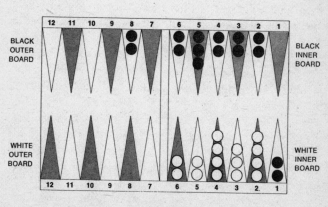

DIAGRAM 7

As you can see, if you get hit now you will have a hard time getting back in, with all the points Black has covered in his inner board. And since you cannot continue to bear off until your man gets all the way around and back into your inner board, you could easily lose. Obviously you do not want to bear off men from the W6 point and the W3 point as this will give Black a shot at the blot on W6. However, you do have an alternative. While you must make every move if you can, you are nonetheless allowed to move within the board if you wish (provided that it is permissible for you to land on that point). Therefore you can take one man off the W6 point and for your three move bring the other man on W6 to the W3 point, so that he is still safe. You have only taken one man off, instead of two, but this is a far wiser move.

Now assume for Diagram 7 that you throw a 6 - 5 (instead of the 6 - 3 we've just discussed). You must take one man off the W6 for the 6 die, but now you cannot move the blot on the W6 point for the five move because the W1 point is covered by Black. You have no choice: you must take a man off the W5 point as well, and now Black has a shot at the two blots on W5 and W6.

Here's another way you can get into trouble: if you do not have a man on the point which corresponds to the number thrown, but do have a man on a higher point, then this man must be moved the proper number of points. Also, if you do not have a man on the point that corresponds to the number thrown, nor do you have one on a higher-numbered point, then you must bear off a man from the highest point on which you have men. Let's assume in Diagram 8 on page 21 that you throw a 6 - 3.

Since you do not have a man on the 6 point, you must take a man off W5 for the 6 throw. The blot you now leave

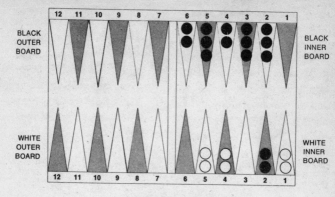

DIAGRAM 8

on W5 cannot move the 3, so you must move a man from the W4 to the W1 point, leaving another vulnerable blot on W4.

Note too that you cannot take a man off the W1 point for the three move, because you still have men on higher points. It is only when you have no men on the point corresponding to the die thrown, or on any higher-numbered points, that you may remove a man from a lower-numbered point than that on the die thrown. And in this case, you then must remove a man from the highest-numbered point you still hold.

This is where a rule I mentioned earlier becomes important. Remember, if you can make one or the other of your moves, but you cannot make both, then the higher one *must* be made. Let's assume in Diagram 9 on page 22 that you roll a 3-1.

Looking at the board, you will see that you cannot make both of your moves. Obviously, if you had a choice, you would make the 1 move bringing the man from W5 to cover the W4 blot. However, since the rule is that you must make

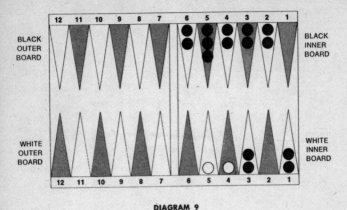

DIAGRAM 9

the higher-numbered move, you *have* to move from the W5 to the W2, thereby still leaving two blots for Black to get a shot at.

Doubles, of course, are played normally even in bearing off: they allow (or require) four moves.

GAMMONS AND BACKGAMMONS

If you succeed in bearing off all of your men before your opponent does, then you have won the game. However, if you do so before he has taken *any* of his men off then you have won a gammon—a double game. Should you be playing for stakes, you have won double the bet. If you should bear off all your men before your opponent has taken any of his men off *and* he still has one or more of his men in *your* inner board or on the bar, then you have won a backgammon— or triple game. And triple the bet.

THE DOUBLING CUBE

Now for the fun, and what this book is all about: betting! Some fifty years or so ago some genius who wanted more action than he was getting with the double and triple game invented the doubling cube. This looks like a refugee from a mah-jongg set, and has on it the numbers, 2, 4, 8, 16, 32, and 64. This is a big gun, and should be treated as such; its principle is to multiply the basic bet and its aim is to annihilate your opponent.

When the game begins you will usually see the doubling cube on the center of the bar, and it is generally turned to 64. This indicates that it really means zero and is up for grabs. (It can be placed off to the side, and left at any number, but the clearest way to use it is as I've indicated. Then there can be no question.) Now, the opening and basic bet is for whatever may have been agreed upon at the outset; let's say a dollar a game. At some point during the play one of the players, thinking he has a sufficient advantage, will turn the cube to the number 2 and place it before his opponent. This is a challenge to double the bet. (Incidentally, the cube can be turned by a player only *before* it is his turn to throw the dice.) The opponent then has the option of accepting the cube and continuing the game, but now for a bet of two dollars, or he can refuse the cube and give up the game, thereby losing the initial dollar bet. If he accepts the double, he keeps the cube on his side of the bar, or he can put it on the table next to his inner board, with the number 2 remaining up. Now, however, the cube is in his control, and only he can throw it the next notch to 4. This may happen if and when the tide of battle turns; a combination of circumstances now places him in what appears to be a strongly advantageous position, and so he turns the cube to 4. The first player now has the option of quitting and paying his opponent two dollars, or accepting and playing for four. If he accepts, the cube of course is now in his control. And so it goes, theoretically as high as the two players wish to take it. In practice, however, it is rare to see it go above 16 or, sometimes, 32.

Finally, the outcome of the game—that is, whether it is a single, double (gammon), or triple (backgammon) game—acts as a multiple of the cube, so that if the cube is at 16, for example, and the game ends as a gammon or double game, the winner has made 32 dollars. Not an uninteresting increase from the initial dollar bet, especially considering that the game has probably taken less than ten minutes to complete! Remember, it is the breakneck speed of the game, once you have learned to play, that gives it so much of its excitement.

A word of caution: *please* don't play for money until you have read more of this book, and especially the chapter on betting. It will not only save you some money, but may also help you make some.

AUTOMATIC DOUBLES

If, in the throw for the first move, doubles are thrown, then each player has to throw his die again. A betting refinement accepted by many players is that this automatically moves the doubling cube up one notch. Of course, it still remains in the center of the table, available to either party; the double has simply doubled the bet.

Also, some players allow the player who gets the higher die on this throw for first turn the option of refusing this combination of dice, if it is not a good one, and throwing both dice over to determine his first move. In some places the doubling cube is also turned up one notch in this case. Both of these points should be discussed and settled before the game begins.

THROWING THE DICE

There are certain basics to be aware of in throwing the dice.

The rules provide that each player throws the dice onto the board on his right, and that if a die jumps the bar, goes off the board, comes to rest on a checker (even if it lands flat) or is tilted in any way, both dice have to be re-thrown.

Although only one pair of dice is necessary to play, it is preferable to use two sets. One reason is that the rules allow a player to change his move, even several times, if he wishes to; picking up his dice is the signal that he has completed his move. When playing with only one pair of dice, the player usually signals the completion of his move by picking them up and handing them to his opponent. Unfortunately, it sometimes happens that the opposing player, in his eagerness, picks up the dice himself before the moves are completed, and in such circumstances I have seen violent arguments ensue as to what the dice said. Having two sets of dice eliminates this problem, since each player touches only his own dice, not his opponent's. When using two sets of dice, if the opposing player should throw his dice before the player making the move picks up his own, he must throw over.

Very often you will also see the dice being thrown from a cup (with two pairs of dice, two cups). The advantage to using a cup is that when the dice are shaken and then thrown from a cup, there can be little if any question about the legitimacy of the roll; when dice are thrown from the hand suspicions may—and sometimes do—arise. I, for one, will never play in a strange place without using a cup.

You will often see players physically counting their move, by pointing or using their index finger to tap out the move on the board. This is a bad habit, and if it is in your repertoire it should be eliminated as soon as possible, simply because it is a dead giveaway that you are a beginner. Psychological warfare is part and parcel of backgammon, and will be discussed in the chapter devoted to strategy. Therefore, as soon as possible learn to count mentally; then, having thought out their ramifications in your mind, make your moves with confidence and assurance.

Also: *always* count the other player's move. Don't assume it is correct. Don't fall into the bad habit of fearing to appear dull by counting the long move. Count mentally if you wish, but check all moves. I won't say that I've seen players cheat, but I have seen games lost because a player made the mistake of not catching a mistake. So don't be shy; count.

INCORRECT MOVES

What about incorrect moves? First, they must be corrected before the subsequent throw of the opposing player. Once this throw has been made, all moves—correct or incorrect—are final. Nor is there an obligation to correct an erroneous move; if your opponent makes a wrong move that is to your advantage, shut up! Not only are you not expected to correct him, but you are considered stupid if you do. This is one game where even the pretenses of "sportsmanship" are eliminated. Outright hostility prevails, and in my opinion the world is better for its being expressed over the gaming board rather than elsewhere.

Of course, if the erroneous move is not in your favor,

point it out. Firmly. I like to add a slight leer when I do; the implication that my opponent may not be quite as smart (or as honest) as I am can sometimes rattle him.

KIBITZERS

The only person who can or should call attention to a mistaken move is the opposing player—not a spectator! It is up to the player himself to keep his opponent honest; third parties, like neutral nations, should not intrude. Unless you are playing a chouette (see Chapter Eleven) backgammon is a head-to-head conflict, and anyone watching the game must remain uninvolved. No comments. No corrections. No grunts of surprise or approval at a play. Nothing. *Just watching.* If a spectator should violate your privacy of play, you have every reason to ask him to respect your rights. He must either remain quiet if he wants to stay and watch, or get a board and partner of his own and play elsewhere. Your manner in firmly dealing with a kibitzer will not only create the proper climate for your game but may also help psych out your opponent by demonstrating your self-assurance and strength of will.

Learn these few rules, then do several things. Read the rest of this book, at least for a general overview. You probably won't get it all at first, but don't panic. There's a lot to assimilate. Try to get someone good to play a few games with you, or go to a pub where backgammon is played; buy a drink and stand around and watch. If you're lucky (I *do* believe in luck) someone will look sympathetic enough for you to question: take advantage of this. You'll quickly begin to understand the complexities—and the fun. The excitement will follow.

Finally, get up the courage to play, which is the only

way to become a good player. Don't worry about making a fool of yourself; the best players often make mistakes, and even more frequently are accused of them.

Very important: as you begin to understand, enjoy, and inquire, go back to specific sections and chapters in this book often. As you get into the game, a lot of the material will take on more meaning and help you to become a good player. Get your money's worth from it.

Then, the supreme test: play for money. Not necessarily much, but enough so that it matters, enough to make you play carefully. I have friends who play for a nickel a point; they'll never really be good because they can afford more. But if they played for a cigarette a point (they are both chain smokers and are constantly running out) they would do much better. You don't make the same mistake a second time when it's costing you. So: play for just a little more than you are willing to lose. But play!

3. IF YOU CAN COUNT TO 36, YOU'RE INTO PROBABILITIES AND ODDS

Probability is the likelihood that a particular event will occur. This is the principle on which thousands of businesses and activities are based, ranging from the mundane one of insurance to the romantic one of space exploration. The application of these principles can be most complex or, as in the case of backgammon, very simple. In either event, probability is a science and, when properly applied in a game, can be of inestimable value in helping you to win. For it is the probabilities that determine the odds, and when you know which move of several is the best one because of the odds of being hit, or because of the odds of covering a blot, then you will be playing backgammon with skill—and for blood!

Of course, luck can be of great importance at any given moment. We have all been in games where you—or your opponent—needed the one great throw, and made it; this can always happen. But I love to play against the man who counts on luck; he is an easy mark for me and for the casinos. The simple fact is that anyone I know who has ever laid claim to a fantastic streak of luck has also forgotten the fantastic streaks of bad luck he has had, both before and after.

However, even when luck is a major factor, you still need as much skill as possible so that you can capitalize on the luck when it comes. In the Super Bowl game, for example, played in deadly earnest with a lot of money at stake for each player, luck is all-important, for both teams are generally so closely matched in skill that it *is* the luck of the fumble, or the interception, or the called-back touchdown, that can make the difference between winning and losing. But the Super Bowl is a one-shot affair. If you're a backgammon player, you will be playing anywhere from ten to fifty games at a sitting, so that you can depend on the luck— a fickle mistress at best—averaging out and the skill of the players becoming of paramount importance. Some players may question this; I have seen them. They are the ones who have had what they explain as a bad run of dice all evening; watching them, I feel that they made some stupid mistakes (maybe only one per game) which became compounded and led to their demise.

If you still believe that luck is all-important and you must depend on it to win, you are wasting your time reading any further. But I would like to play you some day—for lots of money.

There are a few simple principles of probability that

must be understood. A knowledge of them is all that is essential to a consistently skillful and winning game.

First, one must know the total number of possibilities that can occur; mathematicians call this the "sample space." In backgammon, as in craps, the dice can be thrown in a total of thirty-six combinations. There are many backgammon players who will argue avidly that there are only twenty-one, but they are talking about the number of possible *moves*, not the number of possible *throws*.

Assuming an honest die (a cube evenly made, neither weighted nor shaved), the logical and theoretical possibility of rolling any number is equal to that of rolling any other number. That is, all of the six numbers on a die are equally likely to happen. Obviously, if you throw a die only six times, you cannot expect to get each number once (the probabilities of that happening are 1 in 65!). This is because of another law in probability: the law of large numbers. Simply put, you cannot depend on the theoretical probability showing up in a small number of trials. However, the larger the number of throws, the greater the accuracy. What this means to you, therefore, is that the more you play backgammon over a period of time, the more the law of probability will work in your favor.

So, each die can be thrown in six possible ways. If we imagine one die is red and one green, it will be easier to see the results.

Assume the green die comes up 1. The red die can be 1, 2, 3, 4, 5, or 6, for six possible combinations: 1 - 1, 1 - 2, 1 - 3, 1 - 4, 1 - 5, 1 - 6.

If the green die comes up 2, the red die can still be 1, 2, 3, 4, 5, or 6, for another six possible combinations: 2 - 1, 2 - 2, 2 - 3, 2 - 4, 2 - 5, 2 - 6. Note that the move of 2 - 1 can actually be made by a throw of 1 - 2 (green 1 and red 2) or a throw of 2 - 1 (green 2 and red 1). These two throws, although moved identically, are separate and distinct from each other, and contribute individually to the total number of possible throws. Look at Table 1, and you will see this clearly:

Table 1: ALL OF THE POSSIBLE COMBINATIONS THAT CAN BE THROWN WITH TWO DICE

	•	••	••	••	••	••
•	1-1	1-2	1-3	1-4	1-5	1-6
••	2-1	2-2	2-3	2-4	2-5	2-6
••	3-1	3-2	3-3	3-4	3-5	3-6
••	4-1	4-2	4-3	4-4	4-5	4-6
••	5-1	5-2	5-3	5-4	5-5	5-6
••	6-1	6-2	6-3	6-4	6-5	6-6

You will see that there are, in fact, a total of thirty-six possible combinations, without duplication and without overlooking any possibilities. This, then, is the sample space.

From this we can figure how many possible ways each number can be thrown. Unlike craps, where it is the *total* of the two dice that counts, a blot can be hit not only by the total of the two dice but also when the proper number of points shows on either die individually. This is where the craps player often gets into trouble. I have won often against one who was using in backgammon the same odds he would at the craps table, thinking he was using the same dice, only to discover to his chagrin that he had erred more than slightly. In craps, the most probable sum is a 7. It can be rolled six ways: with a 4 - 3, 3 - 4, 5 - 2, 2 - 5, 6 - 1, or 1 - 6. The next easiest sums to roll are a 6 or an 8, each of which can be rolled in five ways. The 6 can be made by a 4 - 2, 2 - 4, 5 - 1, 1 - 5, or 3 - 3. The 8 can be made by a 5 - 3, 3 - 5, 6 - 2, 2 - 6, or 4 - 4. However, in backgammon the 6 can be hit in seventeen ways!—1 - 6, 6 - 1, 2 - 6, 6 - 2, 3 - 6, 6 - 3, 4 -6, 6 - 4, 5 - 6, 6 - 5, 1 - 5, 5 - 1, 2 - 4, 4 - 2, 2 - 2, 3 - 3, and 6 - 6. But the 8 can be hit only six ways: 5 - 3, 3 -5, 6 - 2, 2- 6, 2 - 2, and 4 - 4. The 7 can also be hit in only six ways: 4 - 3, 3 - 4, 5 - 2, 2 - 5, 6 - 1, and 1 - 6. So, the craps player, thinking he is equally safe in backgammon on a 6 point or 8 point, or that he is safer on a 6 point than a 7 point, is very, very wrong!

Table 2 on page 34 shows the total number of ways each number can possibly be thrown:

The odds, should you care to figure them, can then be computed from these two figures. Let's say, for example, you want to know the odds of being hit if you are eight points away. Assuming no intervening points are covered by you, there are six possible ways an eight can be hit, and therefore thirty ways it cannot be hit (the possibilities subtracted from the sample space). The odds against being hit, then, are 30 to 6, or 5 to 1. However, this can be awkward when you try to figure the odds for certain blots. For example, a man nine

Table 2: THE VARIOUS WAYS EACH NUMBER CAN BE THROWN

Shown on the dice:	Number to be hit:																
	1	2	3	4	5	6	7	8	9	10	11	12	15	16	18	20	24
1-1	1	1	1	1													
2-2		1		1		1		1									
3-3			1			1			1			1					
4-4				1				1				1		1			
5-5					1					1			1			1	
6-6						1						1			1		1
1-2 or 2-1	2	2	2														
1-3 or 3-1	2		2	2													
1-4 or 4-1	2			2	2												
1-5 or 5-1	2				2	2											
1-6 or 6-1	2					2	2										
2-3 or 3-2		2	2		2												
2-4 or 4-2		2		2		2											
2-5 or 5-2		2			2		2										
2-6 or 6-2		2				2		2									
3-4 or 4-3			2	2			2										
3-5 or 5-3			2		2			2									
3-6 or 6-3			2			2			2								
4-5 or 5-4				2	2				2								
4-6 or 6-4				2		2				2							
5-6 or 6-5					2	2					2						
TOTAL WAYS:	11	12	14	15	15	17	6	6	5	3	2	3	1	1	1	1	1

points away can be hit in five ways out of thirty-six, which gives you odds of 31 to 5 against being hit. This reduces to a very unwieldy 6.2 to 1. Or try a blot one point away, which can be hit in eleven out of thirty-six ways, for odds of 25 to

11 against being hit. This reduces to 2.272 to 1 against. Why bother? For all practical purposes, it is much easier, faster, and less cumbersome for you to memorize Table 3, and to use this information in a relative way: for example, a blot nine points away can be hit in five ways, whereas one ten points away can be hit in only three ways. In other words, the blot nine points away is almost twice as vulnerable!

The enormous value of this knowledge becomes obvious when you realize the following fact: if you were *not* hit at all, it would require the movement of only seventy-seven points to get all your men into your inner board, ready to bear off. The loss of merely eight points makes your task 10 percent harder and proportionately decreases your possibilities of winning. Conversely, putting yourself in a position where you may be hit and then, in turn, hit back, may be advantageous where you lose only six or seven points and your opponent may lose fifteen or more. Put it another way: each throw of the dice averages a movement of just over eight points (another fact worth remembering); each net loss of eight points consequently puts you one throw behind your opponent. And how many times have you lost by just one throw? (To determine the average movement per throw, add up the value of all 36 throws. This comes to 294; divide this by 36 and you get 8⅙ as the average.)

The knowledge of how many ways a number can be hit, therefore, becomes vital. It affects every move you make, from your opening to bearing off. Therefore, Table 3 on page 36 should be committed to memory.

There is one trap to avoid, which I would like to emphasize here. There is a third rule in probability, called the maturity of the chance. Many times the player who has not rolled a double, for example, in ever so long and now needs one to win, is likely to think that his probability of doing so

Table 3: THE NUMBER OF WAYS A BLOT
CAN BE HIT

A blot	1	point away can be hit	11	ways out of 36
"	2	"	12	"
"	3	"	14	"
"	4	"	15	"
"	5	"	15	"
"	6	"	17	"
"	7	"	6	"
"	8	"	6	"
"	9	"	5	"
"	10	"	3	"
"	11	"	2	"
"	12	"	3	"
"	15	"	1	"
"	16	"	1	"
"	18	"	1	"
"	20	"	1	"
"	24	"	1	"

is increased. This is a fallacy based on the belief that the dice have a memory or a consciousness, and that there is a better chance of a number coming up because it has appeared less frequently than others. This is simply not so: no number has its "share" of the results; there is no equilibrium to be restored. The dice are inanimate; they do not know or take into account any of their previous rolls; *they have no memory.* Each throw of the dice is completely new and individual to itself, and the behavior of the dice is not influenced in the slightest by past throws. The probabilities of the next throw remain precisely the same as they always were before, and as they always will be, no matter what has previously been thrown. What is really valid is the dependability—that is, the probability—of the dice, not their predictability. And it is this dependability that you should know and use.

Now, I could prepare tables that would show how easy or hard it is to hit an opponent's blot when he has intervening points covered, but to me this is a waste of time. I have not memorized this, nor do I intend to; it is too burdensome. The simple rule of thumb is that no matter how many points are covered by your opponent between your man and the blot, the possibilities of hitting do not drop that drastically. If you really must know the relative possibilities, one figure to keep in mind as a basis is: if the blot is anywhere within six points of your man, even if all the intervening points are covered, you always have eleven ways out of thirty-six to hit. As an example, take a blot five points away. If all four of the intervening points are open, you can hit it in fifteen ways. If all the intervening points are covered, you can still hit it in eleven ways: with a 1 - 5, 5 - 1, 2 - 5, 5 - 2, 3 - 5, 5 - 3, 4 - 5, 5 - 4, 5 - 5, 5 - 6, or 6 - 5. So you see that even with all four intervening points blocked by your opponent, the reduction in your chances to hit is only from fifteen to eleven. This is why Table 3 is really all that is important and necessary. Know it cold.

Should you have two places to hit from, you can approximate the possibilities by adding the ways for each to hit; there might be some overlap, but for a quick generalization this will work. And this is also the case even with intervening points covered by your opponent. Take the board in Diagram 10, for example.

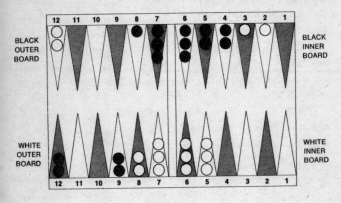

DIAGRAM 10

You can hit the blot on the B8 point in eleven ways from the B3 point, and in eleven ways from the B2 point, which would suggest twenty-two ways of hitting. However, the 5 - 6 and 6 - 5 throws are duplicated, since they work for either blot, and therefore the actual number of throws that will hit the Black blot in this situation is twenty out of thirty-six. For the purpose of the moment it is enough simply to add the two totals.

Want to win a drink as a side bet? Wait till your opponent has a man on the bar, and bet him he doesn't know the chances of entering on his first throw. Very few people do. For example, assume you have three points covered; almost invariably the answer is 50-50. Three points open, three points closed: 50-50. Right? Wrong. The odds are 3 to 1 in favor of his getting in. It's simple. Take this position, for example, although the calculation is exactly the same no matter which three points you cover:

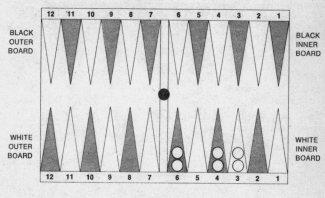

DIAGRAM 11

Only nine throws: 3 - 3, 4 - 4, 6 - 6, 3 - 4, 4 - 3, 3 - 6, 6 - 3, 4 - 6, and 6 - 4, will prevent his entering; the other twenty-seven throws will bring him in. That's 3 to 1 in favor of getting in.

This information about re-entering when you're on the bar is not of value merely to win drinks; it's not an alcoholic's game we're playing. This is information which is important for you when making certain decisions, particularly in connection with the riskiness of blots. Its value will become more and more apparent the more you play and utilize it. Just be sure to keep it in mind.

But if you're a drinking man, you might as well win drinks no matter how many points are covered. For example, with one point covered, many people say it's 5 to 1 to get in on the first throw; same reasoning.

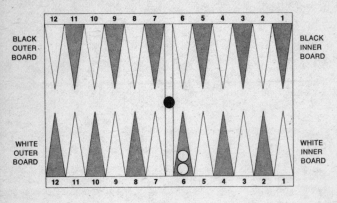

DIAGRAM 12

Actually, it's 35 to 1 in favor; only a double 6 will prevent Black's entry.

With two points covered, the odds in favor are 8 to 1. Again, it makes no difference which two points are covered; the odds are the same. (This is because when entering we do not use the total of the two dice as we do to hit a blot; here it is only the face number of each die that controls.) Assume the 6 and 5 points are the two covered, as in Diagram 13 on page 41.

The man on the bar is prevented from coming in by only four throws: 5 - 5, 6 - 6, 5 - 6, and 6 - 5. All thirty-two other throws are good; the odds, therefore, are 32 to 4 or 8 to 1 in his favor.

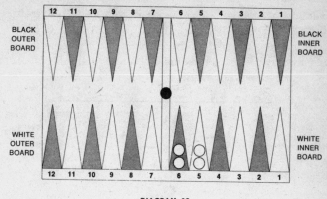

DIAGRAM 13

For four points covered, the odds almost even out. Assume:

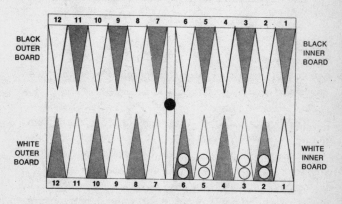

DIAGRAM 14

The man on the bar cannot come in with 2 - 2, 3 - 3, 5 - 5, 6 - 6, 2 - 3, 3 - 2, 2 - 5, 5 - 2, 2 - 6, 6 - 2, 3 - 5, 5 - 3, 3 - 6, 6 - 3, 5 - 6, and 6 - 5; a total of sixteen ways. He can come in in twenty ways, which means the odds are 5 to 4 in his favor.

For five points covered:

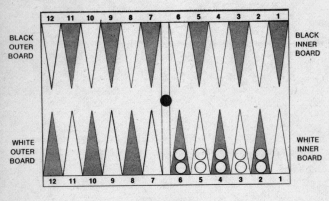

DIAGRAM 15

Black can get in with a 1 - 1, 1 - 2, 2 - 1, 1 - 3, 3 - 1, 1 - 4, 4 - 1, 1 - 5, 5 - 1, 1 - 6, or 6 - 1, for a total of only eleven ways with twenty-five ways no good.

The figures in Table 4 on page 43 are important and should be known.

Although the possibilities of re-entering decrease markedly as more and more points are closed, the really big difference occurs when the fifth point is covered. Not only are the possibilities of re-entering cut almost in half by virtue of this one point, but also there is now less than a 50 percent chance of coming in on the first throw. So I strongly advise

Table 4: THE NUMBER OF WAYS TO RE-ENTER
ON THE FIRST THROW WITH ONE MAN
ON THE BAR:

35 ways to get in with one point covered

32	"	two points	"
27	"	three points	"
20	"	four points	"
11	"	five points	"

great caution once the fifth point is made or seems likely to be made.

With two men on the bar, it obviously becomes much more difficult to bring both men in on the first throw. I won't burden you with the analysis of it; the results are in Table 5 on page 44.

The moral of the information then, is to avoid like the devil having two men hit at once; conversely, it is almost worth selling your soul to put two of your opponent's men on the bar at once.

A few more small pieces of information, and your knowledge of probabilities will be as complete as it need be for your game. (The odds involved in bearing off are treated in Chapter Eight, for that's where they're crucial.)

Table 5: THE NUMBER OF WAYS TO RE-ENTER
TWO MEN ON THE BAR ON THE FIRST THROW

25 ways to get in with one point covered

16	"	two points	"
9	"	three points	"
4	"	four points	"
1	"	five points	"

You may be concerned about a particular combination.
For example, I speak later of the 2 - 1 opener I like:

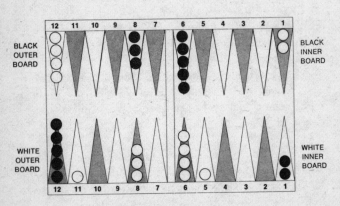

DIAGRAM 16

A 6 - 4 throw by Black is ominous, but there are only two ways out of thirty-six of throwing this combination, or any specific combination, for that matter. So, if you need— or fear—a specific throw, the odds are 34 to 2, or 17 to 1 against its being thrown.

As for doubles, there are six ways out of thirty-six to throw a double, or five to one against throwing one. And to throw a specific double, there is only one way out of thirty-six—or odds of 35 to 1 against throwing it.

The last probability you should know—and as far as I'm concerned the most important one in this book—is not a mathematical probability. However, I can attest to both its validity and value: to lose, all you probably need do is make one mistake.

4. BATTLE STRATEGY:
THE BASIC APPROACH TO WAR

This is not a cookbook. There are no recipes, no suggestions for a pinch of salt. I cannot give you formulas with which to achieve instant success; nobody can. Fortunately, back-gammon is much too complex for this. And that is the fasci-nation: no two games, no two players, are alike. The move-to-move tactics are always different, always new; the battlefield is ever-changing. The game greatly depends on intuition, on feel, on experience—and, of course, on the dice. Therefore, the possibilities, the permutations and combina-tions, are infinite. And so, a book on the details of strategy would be almost as infinite. Actually, there is only one way to be a great player: you have to play and play and play some more, and then begin to formulate your own set of tactics.

What I can give you, however, is a basic approach to overall strategy: ideas that will make you think, help you to experience, and lead you to win. However, you must want to win. That may seem like an obvious statement, but is nonetheless important.

My eleven-year-old daughter, who is a very good player, lost a gammon to me in a game that she thought she had a good chance to pull off. She was furious at both of us (herself for losing, me for winning); she turned on me with venom and blurted out, "I hate you!" I knew then that she would be a great player some day: she had the right attitude.

That's my point. Good guys can win; they simply must have the right attitude. In addition to playing for the fun and excitement of the game, it's all right to be cold-blooded in your approach to winning. You should never feel guilty because you're hated; simply remember that you're playing to win money, not a popularity contest.

Coupled with this compulsive desire to win must be the attitude that you *will* win. I consider this psychological warfare; it is an element that cannot be measured but does, I believe, have incalculable value. An air of cool confidence says it all, and can really rattle an opponent. The way in which you handle your men, how you shake your dice, how you quietly and calmly study the board before making your move, all contribute to this overall attitude. It is the smug smile you wear when you offer a double; it is the speed and assurance with which you accept or refuse it when the cube is thrown at you. In short, it is an attitude which says, "I am a craftsman and a pro, and I shall enjoy taking your money."

Such an attitude may initially serve to make your opponent more cautious, but it will also mean a more challenging—and more interesting—game. In the long run, however, it may also pressure him into making the fatal mistake.

I shall therefore assume that you have both the philosophy of playing to win, and the conviction that you will win. Now let's go on to the strategy necessary to implement this attitude.

Strategy is the science or art of planning the operations of war; since I consider backgammon a battlefield game, this definition of strategy is very appropriate. In this chapter I will discuss the basic strategy with which I play the game, setting it forth in broad concepts, so that you can see the overall pattern. In the next two chapters I will detail the opening and response moves, so that you can see the initial approach to the plan; then, in Chapter Seven, I describe the tactics necessary to implement the strategy as the game progresses. Bearing off and doubling are treated later, in separate chapters.

Most present-day writers on backgammon recommend a running game as their basic strategy: get your men moving as fast as possible out of your opponent's inner board; bring them around quickly; avoid a back game like the plague.

I don't agree.

It is true that you only have to move ten men a total of seventy-seven points in order to be into your inner board and ready to bear off, but if this is what the game is about then all you'd really need do is have each player roll the dice ten times, say, and the one with the highest total would win. Obviously, there's more to backgammon than this; the very derivation of its name (from the middle English *baec* for back, and *gamen* for game or sport) suggests the back game.

I believe there is a simple reason why back games are considered weak: most players accept the philosophy that running is better. Then, when they are caught in a situation where their running game is not winning, or they have been hit several times and have been forced into what they think to be a back game, they are not prepared for it and are fated to lose. What is more, many players have not really learned how to play such a game. Most writers on the subject so strongly emphasize the running game, while making dire predictions of doom about a back game, that the basic fear of such a game and the resultant insecurity in the player becomes a spiraling liability. Consequently, the back game is virtually lost before it is even begun. It is a self-fulfilling prophecy.

Now, let's define a back game, so there is no question about what it is. Basically, a back game is an ambush—except that the player walking into it knows it's there, and where and how strong it is. And the question of whether he's caught by it or not is answered partially by the dice and partially by his knowledge of the probabilities of the dice.

Essentially, a back game is the opposite of a running game. At some point, either because you have been hit frequently and have lost substantial ground, or because your dice have not been good, you find that your position is not as advanced in its forward game as your opponent's. Unless you suddenly get lucky dice—which you can never count on—it is obvious that you cannot win in a straight race. Your only hope, then, is to build either a prime or a side prime (or as much of either as possible) while at the same time obtaining or maintaining a position from which you can subsequently hit one of your opponent's blots. Usually (and ideally) such a position from which to hit is in your opponent's inner board, and so it has come to be called a back game.

For a respectable back game, at least two elements must be present: I must have two of the points in my opponent's inner board covered (or very likely to be covered), and my game has to be sufficiently slowed down so that when I do hit him, he either will be unable to get back in, will be bottled up in my inner board, or will really have to run a gauntlet of my spread-out men, with which I hopefully will continue to hit him.

Now, the basis of the strategy I advocate is that you must plan on the possibility of such a back game from the very beginning, and remain sufficiently flexible so that you can elect this course at your option. You will then have a very good chance to win. Simply put, if you make an early commitment to a running game and then in mid-game are forced to switch to a back game, you are doomed to failure. Conversely, making too early a commitment to a back game is likewise a mistake. I do not advocate either game *per se;* I do recommend that you make no early moves that commit you one way or the other. This is the most important advice I can offer on strategy. (The mechanics of when to decide on a back game, and how best to play it, are set forth in Chapter Seven).

The early tactics involved in the implementation of this strategy depend on position and control; the game I start with is a slow and uncommitted one. Essentially, my prime objective at the beginning of the game is to make strong blocking points, which will serve to bottle up my opponent in my inner board. I love to go for a side prime as soon as possible; I think this is the best way to win. There are two reasons why I think a side prime is preferable to a prime, at least in the early stages of the game. First, if you start making doors on your inner board, such as the 1, 2, or 3 points, these men are effectively out of action for the rest of the game. They cannot be moved to another position of possible strength, as can those men on a point in the outer board; making these forward positions in your inner board too early very often results in having to break up your board. By breaking up your board, I mean a situation in which you have a fairly effective blocking position, but lack sufficient flexibility to make your moves without breaking up these points and destroying the value of this lengthy block.

The second reason is that I want my opponent to break up *his* board. By keeping several of his men bottled up in my inner board, yet allowing him to get back in quickly if I should hit him (either because I want to or have to), I am in effect forcing him to break up his blocking points. This situation can easily evolve if he starts running too fast, I make a few of the blocking points I like, and then manage to hit a blot or two of his. If he can get back in easily, yet finds himself bottled up, he will have to start moving his men to his 1, 2, or 3 points. In this event, I will have no trouble getting back in and around, should he hit a blot I leave. However, there is a danger you should be aware of when this happens: with such a "speed-board," a lucky roll that gets his man (or men) out of my inner board and quickly around might allow him to win because of what has become an excellent board for him to bear off from.

The most valuable points to cover at the beginning of the game are the 5, 7, 9, and 10, in that order; any two of these, together with the 6 and 8 points you start the game with, exert enormous pressure on your opponent, and certainly give you sufficient reason to consider throwing the doubling cube. And if I have managed to cover the three higher blocking points I like (that is, the 7, 9, and 10) I don't even worry too much if he goes to my 5 point. I still have him fairly effectively locked in; but then, when I am ready for it, I also have plenty of room to start getting my men past him and into my inner board without too much danger. I know this is heresy, but try it and see.

When I have a choice, I will generally opt for a builder

in order to make another blocking point rather than run a man merely to make distance. I'm not afraid to take chances and leave men open if there is a possibility that they will be of value if they're not hit; I don't like to make moves to covered points just to keep my men safe and protected. There are those who caution to always cover your blot: leaving a man exposed, they warn, is to announce your masochism and invite certain death. There is some validity to this; having a man sent to the bar can easily set you back two or three throws, and you know how many games are lost by one. But faint heart ne'er won fair lady. There is an element of risk we assume throughout our lives; backgammon merely requires the same. Have the courage to take the risk. Especially early in the game the danger is not great; remember the odds of getting back in. Remember, too, the number of ways blots can be hit; when you have a choice, pick the safer position. As the game progresses, and your opponent's board gets tighter against you, more caution is required. In general, I would advise three considerations when you are leaving a blot: leave it where it is least likely to be hit; leave it where it will be of most value in making a point; or leave it where it presents the greatest threat to your opponent. And, since you're a gambler, gamble. But *with* the probabilities.

I don't believe there is value in having more than three men on any given point at a time; I consider this the right number, in that you can maintain the point and still have a valuable builder or hitter available. I suspect the geniuses who have helped the game evolve to its present structure had this very deliberately in mind when they placed five men on each of two different points. It seems naive to me to think that they should remain there in safety, to be moved only when they can make points; they are really there to be *used* early. For this reason I love a 2 - 1 opener; it's one of the great fun moves of the game. This is my move:

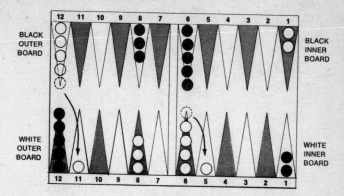

DIAGRAM 17

I'll discuss this move in detail in the next chapter. Not only is it exciting but, more importantly, it is a strong move to implement my strategy of initially going for the blocking points. (If my man on the W5 is not hit, there are thirty-one ways of covering him.) And whenever possible, I use my other openers in the same fashion.

There is a second tactic to be aware of at the beginning of the game; it is the converse of what I've been talking about. The blocking strategy I've proposed obviously works two ways; your opponent can—and may—play the same game. And, obviously, it would be to your advantage to dissuade him from doing so. The most effective way I know to do this is by splitting your back men. This at least doubles the number of ways you can hit any blot he brings into his outer or inner boards as a builder and actually puts enormous pressure on him. For example, another way of playing the 2 - 1 opener (which is also discussed in the chapter on openers) is by moving one man from the B12 to W11 point, so as to have a valuable builder in your outer board, and to move one man from the B1 to the B2 point.

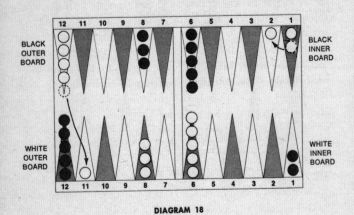

DIAGRAM 18

Look at the pressure you have put on him! You have more than doubled his risk if he moves a builder down to his outer or inner boards; you have also made it more difficult for him to move out of your inner board. Another reason to consider this splitting tactic as an opener is that for certain throws of the dice it is less risky and therefore may be preferable. However, the tactic of splitting weakens the option of readily going into a back game, for the B1 point is a very important one to have if you want to play a back game.

How do you play against such a split on your inner board if your opponent makes it? If the split is to the 4 or 5 points, and I don't have a better move, I generally will hit this blot if I can, even if I leave a blot of my own. Either one of these doors is a good point for me to have, and there is a fairly good chance I can cover either one, even if I have not brought another builder down from my B12 point. Should I be hit, it's still early in the game and easy to get back in; I think it's worth the risk. If the split is to the 2 or 3 points, I will not hit it. The reasons are simple. If I have only one point covered on my inner board (my 6 point), the odds of his coming in on his next throw are 35 to 1. Therefore, I really don't slow him down too much; probably only five points at most, slightly more than half a throw. And the chances of his hitting the inner board blot I've left are 18 out of 36 for the 2 point, and 16 out of 36 for the 3 point. That's almost 1 out of 2. Should I be hit, I will lose at least twenty points, the equivalent of three throws, which is not too appealing. And if I'm not hit, then I have the problem of covering this man, which means two men so far forward they are effectively out of action and have very little—if any—value this early in the game. There is one exception to this; if I throw a double five and my opponent has made the split to the 3 point. This changes things considerably, for now I can hit both of his blots and make two points in my inner board. Remember the odds? They are 3 to 1 against his bringing in both men on his first throw. Should he bring in one or both as blots, I can continue to hit them, and in this situation can probably quickly go into a running game.

How do you choose which of the two approaches to use? Personally, I prefer the blocking tactic to splitting my back men—assuming I have the opening move. Of course, you can—and should—try them both, to see which you're more comfortable with.

If I don't have the opening, but must make the response, my move is based upon certain considerations. Obviously, my first concern is what my opponent has done for his opener; his move may leave me very little choice. I also take into account the kind of player he is. If he generally sits back and primarily goes for his blocking points, I prefer to put the pressure on him that will counter this, knowing that I have somewhat more time to build my own blocking points. Here too, your response will depend to some degree on the style of playing you adopt. I'll discuss this aspect of the game more fully in the chapter on responses.

Bearing these general strategies in mind, then, let us go on to the openers and responses.

5. INSIDIOUS OPENINGS

To have the opening move is of course desirable; you can start playing your kind of game as opposed to merely reacting to your opponent. However, although the probabilities are that you will have the opening move only 50 percent of the time, much of what is said here concerning the strategy you adopt and its resultant tactics at the outset of the game will in many situations function equally well not only for your response but for the first few moves you make as well.

As I have already noted, there are twenty-one working combinations of the dice that govern the moves you make: fifteen throws of the thirty-six possibilities are duplications. And an interesting figure to know is that these twenty-one combinations give you about 350 possible opening moves on the first throw of the dice. (For example, there are fourteen possible moves you can make for the 2 - 1 throw.)

For each of the throws I will give you the moves I recommend, the reasons I like them, an indication of possible alternatives, and why I like them less. Then you can take your board out and juggle your men around; after doing so, I think you may agree with what I suggest. Some of these openers, you will find, are truly insidious.

I find it is clearer to group the moves into several broad patterns based upon the principles involved, instead of taking them in numerical order. It will be easier, too, for you to see and understand them, and then to adopt, adapt, or reject them as you wish.

Certain moves are obvious, and require no discussion. These are 3 - 1, 6 - 1, and 4 - 2.

The 3 - 1 move: For the 3 - 1 move, you should make the 5 point:

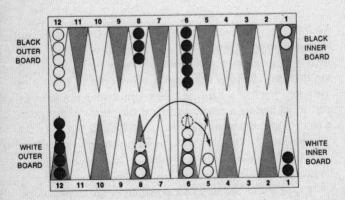

DIAGRAM 19

The 6 - 1 move: For the 6 - 1 move, you should make the 7 point:

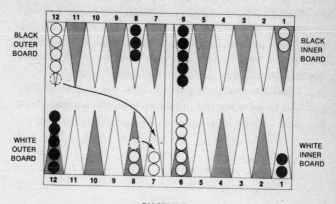

DIAGRAM 20

The 4 - 2 move: For the 4 - 2 move, you should make the 4 point:

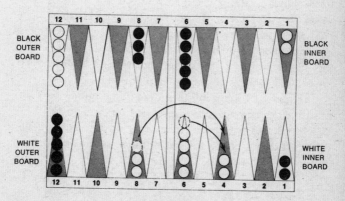

DIAGRAM 21

The next group of openers is what I call the "5 point builder" group. In these moves, which admittedly are adventuresome (but aggressively so), I bring a builder to the W5 point. This is one of the strongest points on the board to hold, and there is a big advantage in making it early. So I go for this immediately if I throw a 5 - 3, 6 - 2, 2 - 1, 4 - 1, or 5 - 1.

This blot on W5 can be hit by your opponent in fifteen ways. But six of these fifteen should give him pause, for they would be beautiful throws if he did not have this dilemma: what does he do if he throws a 1 - 1, 2 - 2, 3 - 1, 1 - 3, 4 - 2, or 2 - 4? These are very good throws for him, but now, with your man on the W5 point, does he use them to make points, or does he hit your blot? It creates certain pressures for him that are hard to resolve; as for you, it means that there are really only nine throws that may hurt you, for I would just as soon see him hit my blot as make the points these throws of his would otherwise allow.

Should your opponent hit you, his inner board is wide open: only a 6 - 6 throw will prevent you from coming back in on your first throw. In addition, having this third man back there places certain pressures on your opponent's outer and inner board builders without necessitating your breaking up the B1 point you cover, and which I think is very important to hold at this early stage of the game.

If your blot is not hit, then even if you do not have an extra builder in your outer board (as you do with the 2 - 1 or 4 - 1 moves), you have twenty-four ways to cover it on your next throw, giving you one of the most valuable points on the board. (You can make the point with a 1 - 1, 2 - 2, 3 - 3, 4 - 4, 2 - 1, 1 - 2, 3 - 1, 1 - 3, 4 - 1, 1 - 4, 5 - 1, 1 - 5, 6 - 1, 1 - 6, 3 - 2, 2 - 3, 6 - 2, 2 - 6, 4 - 3, 3 - 4, 5 - 3, 3 - 5, 6 - 3, or 3 - 6.

Only three of these: 1 - 1, 3 - 1, or 1 - 3 would have made it otherwise.)

Finally, there is no better—or even equally advantageous —move to make with any of these throws; therefore, this is the way to play them.

The 5 - 3 move: For a 5 - 3 throw, I move one man from B12 to W5:

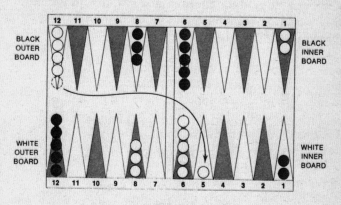

DIAGRAM 22

There are some who advocate making the 3 point when you have a 5 - 3 opener; I don't. This early in the game the 3 point is a waste. It does not really help in blocking your opponent's moves; not until you have made several of the higher-numbered points will this one have value. But making it now will have the disadvantage of effectively removing these two men from action; your mobility will be markedly decreased, and you will soon find yourself in trouble.

Another way of playing the 5 - 3 opener, which is better than making the 3 point but is not as good as the move to the 5 point I've just described, is to move one man from B12 to W8 and one man from B12 to W10:

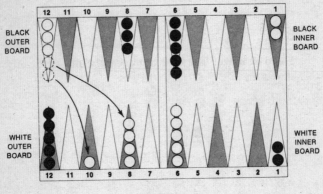

DIAGRAM 23

If you are not hit (there are five ways in which you can be) you then have only thirteen ways to cover the blot on the W10 point, and two of these (the 3 - 1 move) are better utilized to make the W5 point instead. In addition, six other throws are good: a 4 - 1 throw makes the W9 point; a 5 - 1 throw makes W5 point; and a 6 - 2 throw makes the W4 point. So, if we eliminate the 3 - 1 throw from consideration here, there are only seventeen ways to utilize the blot on W10.

Therefore, the comparison for me is this: playing my recommendation, the blot on W5 can be advantageously hit by my opponent in nine ways, and I have twenty-four ways to cover it if it is not hit. Playing the alternative move, the blot on W10 can be hit in five ways, and can be utilized in seventeen ways—but of these, eleven are to make the W10 point, which is not as valuable as the W5 point.

Given the option, I prefer at this early stage of the game to have four men on the B12 point rather than the W8 point; therefore, I consider the move I recommend well worth the risk.

The 6 - 2 move: The 6 - 2 throw can be played exactly the same as the 5 - 3:

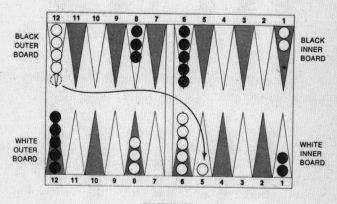

DIAGRAM 24

I've already pointed out the values and consequences to consider if you make the move this way. Later, I'll discuss and compare the alternatives to this throw.

The 2 - 1 move: For the 2 - 1 opener, this is what I do:

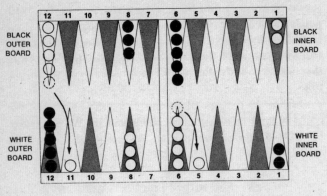

DIAGRAM 25

An alternative to this, which I do not like as much, is to split the back men:

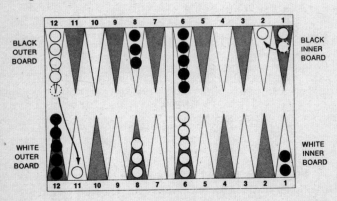

DIAGRAM 26

I like to keep the B1 point intact for several throws, if possible, in order to preserve the option of a strong back game; splitting these back men drastically diminishes this possibility. Remember, the B1 point is the best point on the board to hold for a back game; once you break it and leave a blot on it you can re-cover it only from the bar, and then there are only eleven out of thirty-six ways to do it. Therefore, caution: don't break up this point too soon.

In the 2 - 1 move I recommend, of the nine advantageous ways my opponent can hit my blot on the W5 point, two (6 - 4, 4 - 6) also hit the blot on W11; if this happens I of course may then decide to go into a back game earlier than I otherwise would. However, should my blots not be hit, the chances for me to cover the W5 man are now increased to thirty-one, because of that extra position on W11 from which to make that point! Therefore I love this opener: it's almost foolproof.

The 4 - 1 move: The 4 - 1 opener is treated the same way: move a man from B12 to W9 and a man from W6 to W5:

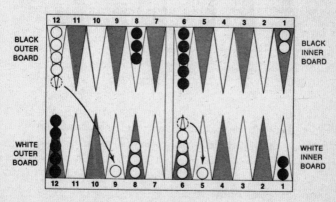

DIAGRAM 27

There are nineteen ways that one or the other of my two blots can be hit (the fifteen ways to hit the W5, plus 5 - 3, 3 - 5, 6 - 2, and 2 - 6); only one (a 4 - 4 throw) can hit both. Again, six of these throws would keep my opponent from making an otherwise strong move. And there are now twenty-nine ways in which I can cover the W5 blot if I am not hit. Therefore, here too the move is very well worth the risk.

The 5 - 1 move: Of the group of 5 point builders, the 5 - 1 opener is the least valuable:

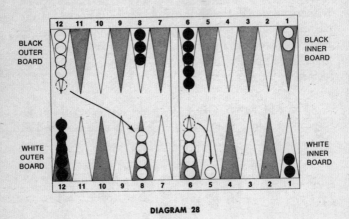

DIAGRAM 28

Although I don't like bringing another man to the W8 point this early in the game, this point is so important for building that this fourth man on it will be of future value. The ramifications of the blot on W5 being hit and being covered have already been discussed; this move is the best possible one for this throw.

We now get into the group of moves I call "two builders": they are 3 - 2, 4 - 3, 5 - 2, and 5 - 4. Even though I do not like to deplete the B12 point this early in the game, bringing two men down from this point to serve as builders is the best way to handle any of these throws. Let's take them in turn.

The 3 - 2 move: For the 3 - 2 move, you should bring two men from B12 to the W10 and W11 points:

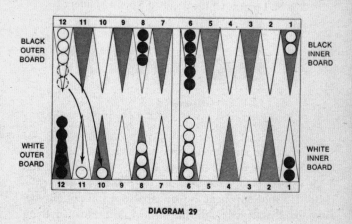

DIAGRAM 29

There are only seven ways in which your opponent can hit one of your blots (5 - 4, 4 - 5, 6 - 3, 3 - 6, 6 - 4, 4 - 6, and 3 - 3); if he does hit you with the 3 - 3 throw it obviously destroys a strong move he could otherwise make. And, should neither blot be hit, you then can make one good point or another with *any* throw except a 5 - 4! You can't ask for more; it's a very good move for a mediocre throw.

The 4 - 3 move: For the 4 - 3 throw, you should bring two men from B12 to the W9 and W10 points:

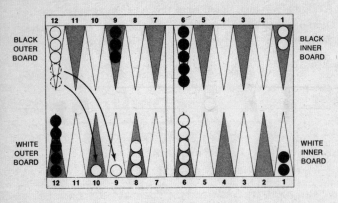

DIAGRAM 30

Here there are eleven ways in which you can be hit: 2 - 2, 3 - 3, 4 - 4, 6 - 2, 2 - 6, 6 - 3, 3 - 6, 5 - 4, 4 - 5, 5 - 3, and 3 - 5; two of them (the 2 - 2 and 3 - 3 throws) are really better for your opponent to play otherwise and not hit you. Here too, should you not be hit, on your next throw anything except a 5 - 2 will allow you to make a valuable point.

Some authors recommend making your 4 - 3 move as shown in Diagram 31 on page 69, splitting your back men:

I advise against this for several reasons. First, I do not want to break up the B1 point this early (for reasons I have already discussed), especially since I would not be gaining any discernible advantage. Second, the blot on B5 can be hit in twenty-three ways, which not only puts it back on the bar but allows my opponent a builder on this important

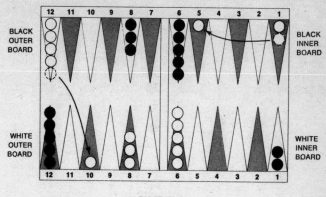

DIAGRAM 31

point. Should the blot be hit, I can then hit my opponent's blot in twenty-one ways, which is an advantage in the trade-off; however, in either event I have the subsequent problem of how to deal with this man. If I don't move him, he remains vulnerable, and on a point I don't want my opponent to build on or cover. And if I do move this man, he really can't do me any practical good on his next move; his only immediate value, then, is to serve as a threat against my opponent's bringing a builder down into his outer board. Therefore I don't like this move as much as the one I recommend for this throw.

The 5 - 2 move: Here, as in Diagram 32 on page 70, the initial possibilities are not as broad:

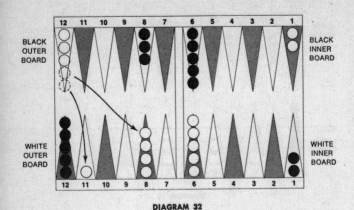

DIAGRAM 32

The man from B12 to the W11 point is of value, but the man from B12 to W8 is at this moment merely a reinforcement for future building (unless you get a 1 - 1 or 3 - 3 throw next, in which case having this extra man on W8 really helps). The man on W11 can be hit in only two ways (6 - 4 and 4 - 6)—not much of a risk. And on your next throw this builder can be utilized in thirteen ways, while eleven other throws also make points. Not as strong a move as the others in this group, but still the best one for this throw.

The 5 - 4 move: This is in the same category as the 5 - 2 move in terms of the B12 man to W8 being a reinforcement rather than of immediate potential; the move is shown in Diagram 33 on page 71.

The blot on W9 can be hit in only six ways (2 - 2, 4 - 4, 6 - 2, 2 - 6, 5 - 3, and 3 - 5), but it would be a waste for your opponent to use the 2 - 2 or 4 - 4 throws by hitting you. If

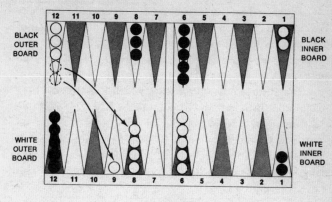

DIAGRAM 33

not hit, the W9 man can be utilized in twenty-one throws, and five others make points as well.

For this opener, the author who recommended splitting the back men for the 4 - 3 move advises doing the same thing here:

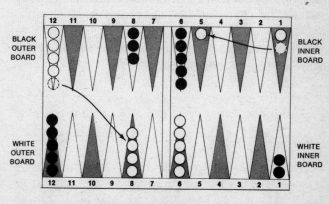

DIAGRAM 34

Again, and for the same reasons, I disagree. In fact, here the move is even worse, since this has the disadvantage of four men on the W8 point and no additional building point in your outer board as there was with the 4 - 3 move he suggests.

There is one other alternative, which I also do not like: to move one man from the B1 point to the B10. This has three disadvantages: it breaks up the B1 point; it is of no use on your next throw except for a 6 - 4 or 4 - 6; and because it can be hit in thirteen ways it really has to be removed from danger on your next throw if it is not immediately hit. This move is a liability; avoid it.

We now come to what I consider the most interesting group of opening moves; I call them the "six plus" throws. These are 6 - 3, 6 - 4, and 6 - 5. What I suggest may seem sacrilegious; still, I urge you to trust me and try them anyway. Watch your opponent's eyebrows when you make one of these moves. If he hasn't read this book I almost guarantee they will arch. But then watch the moves play out; they really are insidious. And you may find that you like them.

The 6 - 3 move: For this move I bring two men down from the B12 point, as in Diagram 35.

The W7 can be hit in seventeen ways (2 - 2, 3 - 3, 6 - 6, 4 - 2, 2 - 4, 5 - 1, 1 - 5, 6 - 1, 1 - 6, 6 - 2, 2 - 6, 6 - 3, 3 - 6, 6 - 4, 4 - 6, 6 - 5, and 5 - 6), but of these there are six throws (2 - 2, 3 - 3, 6 - 1, 1 - 6, 4 - 2, and 2 - 4) that your opponent would otherwise be able to use very effectively, and so he must stop to consider whether or not to hit you or play them as he should. Since it really hurts him to not make his points with

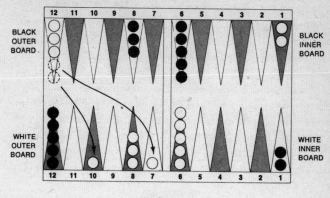

DIAGRAM 35

them, there are only eleven effective throws against this blot. Of course a 6 - 3, 3 - 6, or 3 - 3 throw hits both blots, and a 5 - 4 throw hits the blot on W10. I consider this to be a total of fourteen throws that can hit you. Against this is the potential on your next move if you are not hit: every single throw of the dice except the 5 - 4 will make one point or another! (Even the 5 - 4 will allow you to make the W3 point, but I would still prefer not to make it, and so am not counting this as a possibility.) Some of these throws will make points without using these builders; if so, their potential (as builders) remains for your next throw as well. But isn't it an exhilarating feeling to know that on your next throw virtually anything you roll will make a point?

Other authors have different recommendations for this move. One of them runs a man from B1 to B10:

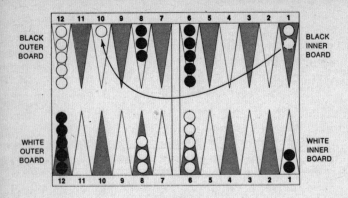

DIAGRAM 36

Another author moves one man from B12 to W10 and splits the back men by moving one man from B1 to B7:

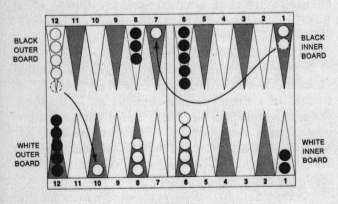

DIAGRAM 37

I don't like either.

Primarily, I have, as noted, a basic objection to breaking

up the B1 point so early in the game. But there are other disadvantages to these alternatives.

As for the first suggestion, the move to the B10 point, I have the same objections here as I did to this move for the 5 - 4 throw: it is of no use on your next roll, except for a 6 - 4; and because the blot is so vulnerable it must quickly be removed from danger.

As for the second suggestion, it is even worse: it leaves the B7 blot vulnerable not only to being hit in seventeen ways, but also gives your opponent a builder on a point that is very important for him to cover early if he can. So, if he hits you there, he is fully utilizing any 6 throw he gets, and he has none of the disadvantages of doing so. Should you be hit, and should your opponent not cover this blot simultaneously, you have only sixteen ways of coming in and hitting him in turn, and even then you are merely achieving the same disadvantageous position from which you were just forcibly ejected.

Further, this move commits you almost irrevocably to your next move. For if the blot is not hit (or if it is hit and you hit your opponent's blot in turn), you cannot leave it uncovered on this point. To do so is suicide. Once you move to B7, you are committed to either covering it (thereby virtually foregoing any option for a back game) or getting out of there fast—and then its only immediate value accrues if you throw a 5 - 3, 3 - 5, 6 - 2, 2 - 6, or 4 - 4, any of which would allow you to cover the blot on W10. Other throws would either bring this blot to safety, or put it into another position of vulnerability—and neither situation is particularly desirable.

The argument sometimes made in favor of these alternatives is that they start your running game. This is not only specious reasoning but is, in fact, dangerous: it gets you running *too* early. And in terms of forward progress *per se*, the practical measurement is in terms of getting your men into your inner board; it makes no difference for this purpose which of your men do the running at any given moment as long as the moves are not wasted. Consequently, when you are talking about "forward progress," one man moved nine points from B1 to B10 does not achieve this purpose any faster than two men moved six points and three points respectively from the B12 point.

An argument in favor of the second alternative that might be more reasonably advanced is that if the W7 blot is hit, you are set back eighteen points, whereas if it is the B7 blot that is hit you are only set back seven points. However, when weighed against the other considerations, this eleven-point differential is not as valuable to me as the potential advantages of being on the W7 point.

Everything I have said about the 6 - 3 move applies to both the 6 - 4 and 6 - 5 moves.

The 6 - 4 move: I recommend this:

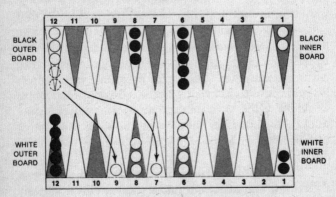

DIAGRAM 38

Other authors recommend the following. (One of them is often inconsistent; with the 6 - 3 throw he moved one man from B1 to B7 and one from B12 to W10, yet here he does not bring a man to B7 and another to W9. I don't know why.)

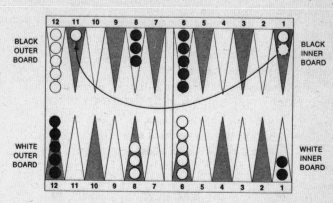

DIAGRAM 39

In this alternative move, although the blot on B11 can be hit in fewer ways (eleven) than if he were on B7, he is of no practical advantage except to team up with a man from B12 to make a point; only a 5 - 4, 4 - 5, 4 - 3, 3 - 4, 3 - 2, or 2 - 3 allows this. And if not so utilized, he must be moved out of danger shortly. Thus, for this alternative, there are many problems—and no advantages.

As for my recommendation, the blot on W7 can be hit in seventeen ways (remember, though, six of them are not advantageous for my opponent), the W9 blot can be hit in three ways (5 - 3, 3 - 5, and 4 - 4), and the 6 - 2 or 2 - 6 throws hit both blots. Practically speaking, that means a total of sixteen ways to be hurt. But if I am not hit, then on my next throw of the dice I am again in great shape: *any throw at all* will somehow make a point. Seemingly incredible, but true! If you doubt me, go back and look at the diagram again.

The 6-5 move: For the 6-5 move, I bring two men from B12: one to W8 and one to W7.

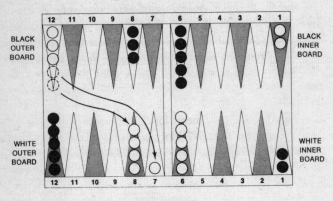

DIAGRAM 40

Other authors recommend moving one man from B1 to B12:

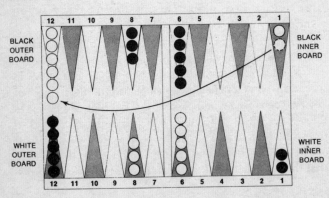

DIAGRAM 41

This alternative is called "lover's leap," though no one seems to know why. I pondered this for a long time, and then it suddenly dawned on me: a lover's leap is a death jump, and that's exactly what this is. Play this throw in this fashion, and you are virtually destined to doom. Not only do you have the disadvantage of breaking up your B1 point, but also the handicap of effectively immobilizing yourself: you have no flexibility. Six men on the B12 point is a hazard; the only faintly reasonable claim for this move is that your man is "safe." True, but so what? Not only is this a game that will be very hard to win, but it also is going to be very dull and plodding, and too often you will find yourself at the bottom of the cliff.

The move I recommend for this throw is surprising in its statistics: here, the W7 blot can be hit in the seventeen ways I've talked about before; six of these, you will recall, are at the expense of what would otherwise be a strong move for your opponent. But against this, thirty of your throws on your next turn will make a point, and four more of them (5 - 3, 3 - 5, 5 - 4, and 4 - 5) will even make the W3 point, if you want to cover it this early. (Only the 5 - 2 or 2 - 5 throws do nothing.) These are very good odds in your favor, and it's well worth making the move this way—even if the alternative was not as bad as it is.

You may ask why I don't play the 6 - 2 throw the same way I do the other "six plus" moves. It's because I would rather make the W5 point than the W7, and when you compare the two moves and see how close they are in their probabilities, you can understand my choice. Here is the comparison:

The move from B12 to W5 leaves the blot vulnerable in fifteen ways, of which six are disadvantageous to my opponent, and it can be covered in twenty-four ways. If I subtract the effective probabilities of being hit (nine) from the ways it can be covered (twenty-four), I have a net value of fifteen.

The move of one man from B12 to W7 and one man from B12 to W11 leaves the W7 blot vulnerable in seventeen ways, of which six are debatable for your opponent; two of the eleven remaining also hit the blot on W11 as well. There are twenty-nine ways to cover the W7 blot, plus two ways (3-2, 2-3) to make the W5 point using this blot. Here, the effective hitting probabilities (thirteen) subtracted from the ways it can be used (thirty-one) leave me a net value of eighteen; there is not that much difference between this move and the one I prefer.

In addition, there is one other small value in the move I recommend, and for me this clinches it. My move still leaves four men on B12, as opposed to three if I bring two men down from it, and I like the flexibility of that fourth man still on B12 this early on.

Therefore, I play the 6-2 move by bringing one man from B12 to W5. But if you want to play it the alternative way I've discussed, that too is a very strong move.

The final group of moves to discuss is doubles, since many people play contrary to the rules of the International Backgammon Association and allow the person who throws the higher die to re-cast both dice for his initial move. And, of course, as with the other moves suggested in this chapter, very often the recommendations for openers will serve equally well either for the reply move, or for a move somewhat later in the game.

The 1 - 1 move: For this throw, move two men from W6 to W5 and two men from W8 to W7:

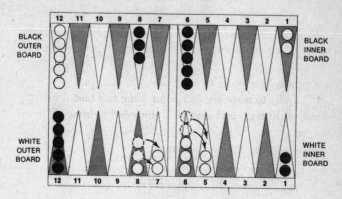

DIAGRAM 42

There is no viable alternative to this move. It is a strong opener, even though it breaks up the valuable W8 point. The blot left there can be hit in only six ways (6 - 1, 1 - 6, 5 - 2, 2 - 5, 4 - 3, or 3 - 4); but if it is not hit and you cover it on your next throw (fifteen ways to do this) you probably can either throw the doubling cube or even go for a gammon.

The 2 - 2 move: For this throw, there are two alternatives I like very much. When you get this throw, play a few games each way and see how you feel. The first is to move two men from the W6 point to W4 and two men from B12 to W11:

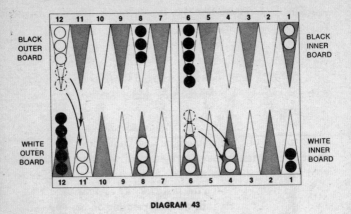

DIAGRAM 43

The second is to move two men from B12 to W9:

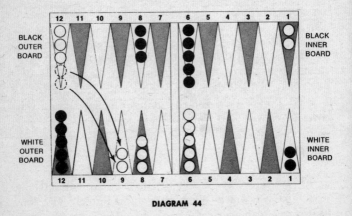

DIAGRAM 44

The first alternative has these advantages: it utilizes
two men from the heavy W6 point to make another im-

portant point, and it also brings two men down to your outer board where, in addition to giving you a valuable point from which to build, they exert an additional pressure on your opponent when he tries to run from your inner board. However, the W11 point is two points too far from the W4 point to be of value in a potential side prime, and so it is only of temporary value.

The second alternative has the advantage of making a point that is of both immediate and continuing value; this point is important enough to hold until you start closing up your inner board. Also, in terms of forward progress, it fully utilizes the throw, which the first alternative does not.

I play this throw both ways, depending on my opponent. If he is a cautious player and does not give me much opportunity to hit him, I am not as concerned about closing the W4 door too early. If he is a more open player and takes chances more freely, I then make the point. In doing so, when I hit him I have reduced the chances of his getting in on his first throw from 35 to 1 to 8 to 1, a very substantial drop.

I have also seen this used for the 2 - 2 throw:

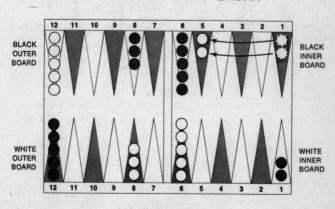

DIAGRAM 45

I don't like this at all. The value of holding the B1 point to keep open your option to go into a back game has already been discussed; further, if you make this move you have not increased the pressure on your opponent's men in your inner board. Forget this alternative; play this throw either of the other two ways.

The 3 - 3 move: My recommendation for this throw is also rather novel; none of the other writers suggests playing it this way, but I think it's a great opener. On a 3 - 3 throw, I move two men from B12 to W10 and two men from W8 to W5.

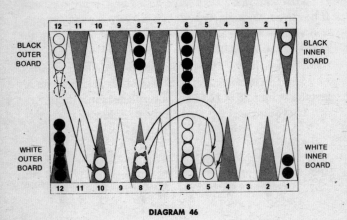

DIAGRAM 46

One alternative sometimes suggested is to move two men from W8 to W5 and two men from W6 to W3:

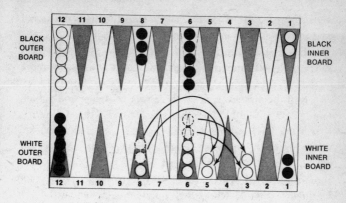

DIAGRAM 47

A second alternative is to move two men from B1 to B4 and two men from W8 to W5:

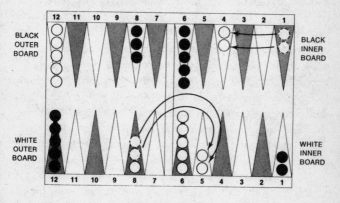

DIAGRAM 48

Let me dispose of this last one first. I dislike it for the reason I have by now made very obvious: I do not want to move from the B1 point this early. And the B4 point is not a strong one to hold in any event.

The first alternative suggested (W8 to W5 and W6 to W3) is a good one, and superficially may even seem more attractive, yet I think my recommendation is preferable.

Both boards are well on their way to being side primes (mine W5 through W10, the alternate W3 through W6), with each having three points covered and a blot on W8. However, the W3 point is actually not very much of an asset at this time. It is not a difficult one to pass, and the men there are, for all practical purposes, out of play. This point is chiefly valuable when your opponent has a man on the bar and, even then, with three points covered against him, he still has a 3 to 1 chance of getting in on his first roll.

On my board, having the W10 point covered gives you tremendous flexibility. These two men are still mobile, if and when you need them. They immediately give you an extra position from which you can build if it is really advantageous, although the value of this point is enhanced by not breaking it up too soon. You have also established another salient base of safety; refuges of this sort can be very important. Further, you have another position from which to hit your opponent's blot coming out of your inner board, and consequently it acts somewhat like a protecting "Big Brother" to your exposed man on W8, making it more dangerous for your opponent to hit you there than if he hits the same blot on the alternative board.

Another substantial advantage of my recommendation is that you have moved six points closer to your inner board (of the total of seventy-seven you need), and thus enhanced your offensive game while at the same time strengthening your defensive game. It's nice to have both advantages coincide.

Convinced? If not, be secure in the knowledge that the alternative is, as I said, a good one as well.

One other possibility I'd like to mention is to move two men down from B12 to W7:

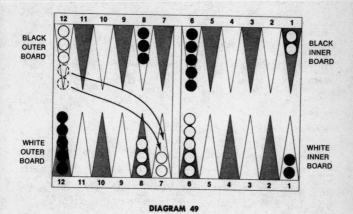

DIAGRAM 49

I don't like this move as much, simply because it does not place the same pressure on your opponent that the other two possibilities do. I therefore do not recommend it.

The 4-4 move: There are several ways to play this throw. The move I recommend is to bring two men from B12 to W5:

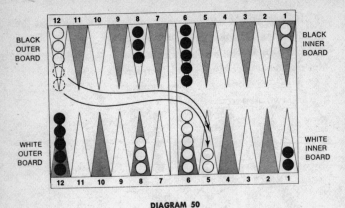

DIAGRAM 50

This makes a very important point; it leaves you builders (without exposure) on W6, W8, and B12; and it greatly enhances your blocking game. It is extremely strong.

The first alternative is to move two men from B12 to W9 and two men from W8 to W4:

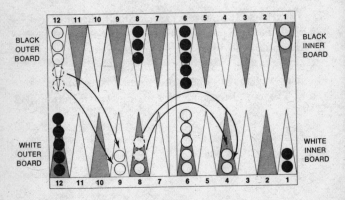

DIAGRAM 51

This is almost as good, and has many of the same advantages that the similar move for the 3 - 3 opener has. I don't think you'll be making a mistake to play it this way. It is a matter of preference, and I prefer the W5 point.

A second alternative is to move two men from B12 to W9 and two men from B1 to B5:

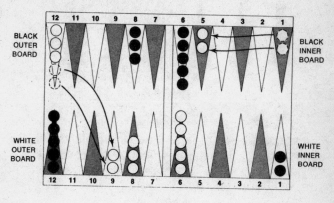

DIAGRAM 52

Here again, I don't like this early a move from the B1 point, and I recommend against it.

Another alternative I've seen used is to run the two men on B1 all the way out to B9, as shown in Diagram 53 on page 90.

In this move you are totally committed to a running game and had better start praying. Further, you have done nothing to improve your blocking position. This is the weakest of the various alternatives for this throw.

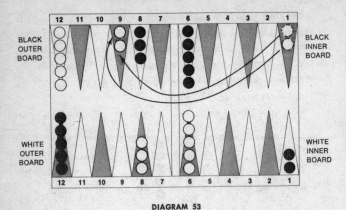

DIAGRAM 53

The 5 - 5 move: There is only one possible way to play this throw; it's not a particularly good move but you have no choice. You move two men from B12 to W3:

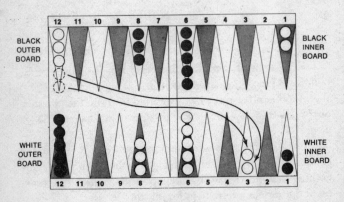

DIAGRAM 54

Because you now have fewer alternatives with which to build a blocking board, you are not in as good a situation to opt for a back game, and your strategy after this opening should be more geared to a running game. I don't like to have this forced on me, but you can't fight the dice.

The 6 - 6 move: Here too there is no choice as to your move: it's two men from B1 to B7 and two men from B12 to W7.

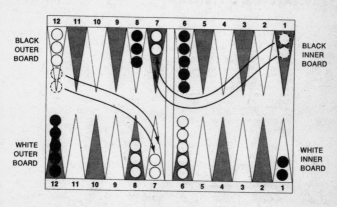

BLACK OUTER BOARD

BLACK INNER BOARD

WHITE OUTER BOARD

WHITE INNER BOARD

DIAGRAM 55

Here, even more than with the 5 - 5 opener, you are virtually committed to a running game since you no longer hold a point in your opponent's inner board. Therefore, play cautiously and try not to get hit; you have moved almost a third of the total forward game you need, and you should try to make the most of it.

So much for openers. Now, on to responses.

6. RETALIATIONS: REPLIES OF CONSEQUENCE

The reply move cannot be as simplified a statement as is the opener; even if you accept the moves I have recommended for the opening throws there would have to be 441 responses shown in order to be complete. (There are twenty-one opening moves, and for each individual one there are twenty-one responses—for a total of 441.) Unfortunately, this complexity, which is one of the fascinations of backgammon, is both beyond the realm of this book and (probably) the scope of your patience. However, there are several broad considerations involved that make this discussion less complicated than it may appear.

To begin with, in some situations the move recommended for the opener will be the obvious one for the reply as well. For many of your throws—the doubles, 6 - 1, 3 - 1, and 4 - 2—you probably can and should play it the same way you would if it were your opener. Remember that your initial strength comes from the blocking points I discussed; it is a strategy of position that pays great dividends as the game progresses. This is a basic principle to follow; your primary concern should be to make these blocking points as early as possible.

Sometimes, because of your opponent's opener, this will be even more fortuitous; the combination of his opening and the dice you have thrown may allow you to make a very strong move. For example, suppose your opponent throws a 6 - 2 for his opener and splits his back men like this:

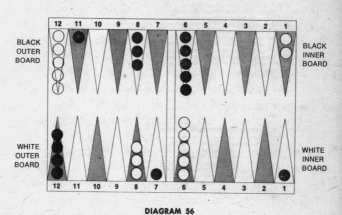

DIAGRAM 56

If you then throw a 6 - 1, your obvious move has the added advantage of hitting his blot too. When this happens, it's nice not to have had the opening move.

Let's stay with this situation for a moment, where your opponent has split his back men and brought a man out to your 7 point. This man should be hit if you can do so; your response may accordingly be changed somewhat from the suggestion for the opener. For example, I'd hit him with a 4 - 2 throw instead of making the W4 point; the combined value of setting him back and putting a builder on the very valuable W7 point compels this move. In fact, you should hit this blot with anything you throw that shows a 6, and also with anything that shows a 1 (except the 3 - 1). Although in my discussion of openers I explained the advantages, on a 2 - 1, 4 - 1, or 5 - 1 throw, of moving a man from the W6 point to the W5, rather than W8 to W7, now, of course, the situation is different, and you should hit this blot. Putting him back on the bar is worth the difference of placing the builder on the lesser point. With this man on the bar, and the blot on W1, he can enter and hit your man on W7 in only seventeen ways; slightly less than a 50 percent chance. But if he does not hit you, then your chances of covering this man, or at least making a point, are thirty ways out of the thirty-six if your initial throw had been a 5 - 1, thirty-two ways if your initial throw had been a 2 - 1, and *anything* you throw will make a point if your initial throw had been a 4 - 1!

What I've enunciated here is a second principle to follow: in general, hit your opponent when you can, especially when it also either helps you in achieving a position or when it serves to protect you. Even if you forego a move you would prefer to make, hitting him and setting him back has considerable value; remember that every eight points he loses is the equivalent of one throw.

This principle should always be followed if he runs one of his back men to your outer board, beyond W7. Here, hitting him not only will set him back at least a throw, but it also serves to bring a builder down for you. I would not recommend doing so at the expense of making a valuable point, but hitting him anywhere within your outer board is certainly the second priority. With a man on the bar, and a blot on W1, there are only five ways your opponent can come in and also hit your blot on W9; three ways he can do so if you are on W10, and only two ways if you are on W11. So it obviously presents little danger if you hit him in your outer board. (I've already mentioned that there are seventeen ways if you are on W7; this risk is also worth taking.)

If he splits his men in your inner board, I generally don't recommend hitting him unless you can cover the point as well. This is because you will not really slow him down by hitting him if you have only one point covered in your inner board, and he has eighteen ways of coming back in and hitting you if you are on the W2 point, nineteen ways of doing so if you are on W3, twenty ways if you are on W4, and twenty-one ways if you are on W5. And if you are not hit on his next throw, you then have the problem of having to cover this blot on your next throw; otherwise it remains vulnerable. The W2 and W3 points have the additional disadvantage of being too far advanced for this early in the game, thus hindering your mobility.

As for the W4 and W5 points, the chances of his hitting you back, should you hit him there, are strongly in his favor (twenty and twenty-one, respectively), and therefore I suggest that you generally avoid this if there is a better move you can make. However, if your throw would otherwise dictate a blot in your outer board, you should keep in mind certain figures.

If he has men on W1 and W5, as in Diagram 57 on page 96, for example, he can hit a blot you place on W7 in twenty-three ways, and a blot you place on W9, W10, or W11 can be hit in sixteen ways. But if you hit him on W5 (with a 6 - 2, say) he can re-enter and hit you back in only twenty-one ways; you are obviously better off to hit him under these circumstances. And if he does not hit you in turn, you then have twenty-four ways in which to make this point. It's a good move; it's also infinitely better to do this than to move to B7, in case you are thinking about splitting your back men in that fashion.

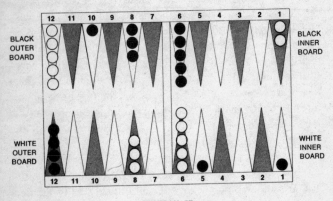

DIAGRAM 57

If his split should be to your W4 point, so that he has men on your W1 and W4 points, as in Diagram 58, and the situation is the same as I've just described (you have the choice of hitting him or bringing a builder down to your outer board), you should hit him here as well.

Here are the figures: if you put a blot on W5, it can be hit in twenty-one ways; a blot on W7 can be hit in twenty-seven ways; a blot on W9 can be hit in nineteen ways; a blot on W10 can be hit in eighteen ways; and a blot on W11 can be hit in eight ways. If, instead, you hit him on W4, he can re-enter and hit you in turn in twenty ways, almost equal in

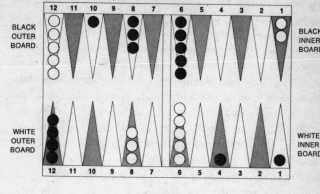

DIAGRAM 58

chances to that of a blot on W5, W9, or W10, and certainly much less risky than putting a blot on W7. Therefore, in this situation, you should hit him on the W4 point as well.

My third priority is to try to keep my B1 point intact, at least initially; I try not to break it up unless there is a distinct need to do so. Generally, on this reply move, I do not hit a builder he may bring down to his outer board, unless it is to his B7 or B9 points. Here the chances of his making a valuable point are so good that I generally must prevent it as a matter of self-preservation. However, even here if there is a better move for me, I will make it; it is only with the utmost reluctance that I break up this point.

But if my opponent puts a builder on his B5 point, I will invariably hit it; this point is too valuable to him, and the chances of his covering it are too good for me to allow the insolence. Bang! (If I can.)

There is no conceivable way he would have a blot on

B4, B3, or B2 on his opening move; therefore we need not consider these.

Finally, if your opponent should throw a 6 - 1, 3 - 1, 4 - 2, or a double, and makes one or more blocking points, there is a tendency on the part of many players to panic and start running a back man. The theory is that you have to get him to safety as soon as possible. Don't. Don't panic; don't run. This is precisely the time when you should cherish the security of having the B1 point covered. You may be closer to a back game than you think, in which case you need this point. And having it allows you to become even a little more flagrant in your moves; if you do not get away with a particularly daring move, you can go into the back game relatively easily and well.

With these principles in mind, then, you should be in good shape even if you don't get the opening move.

7. BATTLE STRATEGY: TACTICS DURING THE GAME

Of course, nothing is sacred, not even my advice. Although I strongly recommend as gospel that you stay in a game of position and control and keep your options open until well into the mid-game, you really have to play the dice—and your opponent. Together they determine your movements and consequently your game to a great extent. Therefore you have to be flexible, ready to adopt, adjust, and shift strategies as the vagaries of the game require.

For example, there really is no choice in the matter if I throw a double 6 and my opponent throws a 2 - 1, splitting his back men, so that the board looks like this:

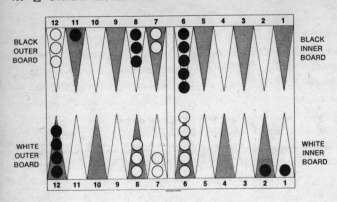

DIAGRAM 59

If I throw a double 5, I'm running, period. Virtually anything I then throw in this situation puts me into a very good running game. In fact, half of the possible throws even encourage me to double on my next turn if my opponent doesn't make a great toss. The point is that your tactics may at times be determined for you; you may have no control. And they can just as easily be changed often during the game; even one throw can sometimes be crucial. Therefore, you have to constantly examine the board to determine when a change in the balance occurs. The ability to quickly evaluate your position vis-à-vis your opponent's is obviously of paramount importance. I say "quickly" because in playing you can't—or at least don't—take the time to ponder forever. The (unspoken) pressure is great; decisions must be made, and made quickly, or you'll start losing playing partners with as much certainty as if you have bad breath. Moreover, there is the practical requirement of simplicity, for it is imperative that your evaluation system be so easy and accurate that you will not make a tragic error under the pressure of play.

My basis for deciding on my course of action is an estimate of the number of throws probably necessary for each of us to get into our inner boards and begin bearing off, and a consideration of this in relation to the lateness of the game. I find this method of counting to be the most practical, for it is the number of throws that usually decides a game. My most vivid memories are of those games I won—or lost—by one throw.

At this mid-game time, you should disregard the number of throws necessary to bear off, as it simply complicates the thinking. Once you begin to bear off it becomes important, and can also affect the matter of doubling. (Both bearing off and doubling will be discussed in chapters Eight and Nine.) But here, when it is still fairly early in the game and there are men to be brought into the inner board, for the purpose of evaluating relative positions it is reasonable to assume that the number of throws necessary to bear off once you are in the inner board will be the same for both of you. Also, in counting the number of throws, you can disregard the possibility of doubles, for your chances of getting them are the same as your opponent's.

Since the average movement of each throw is eight points, count any of your men that are in your outer board, or on Black's 11 or 12 points, as requiring one throw to get in. Any man on Black's 3 through 10 points will require two throws. And a man on Black's 1 or 2 points will require three throws. A man on the bar is at least three throws, possibly more, depending on the number of points covered, as shown in Diagram 60 on page 102:

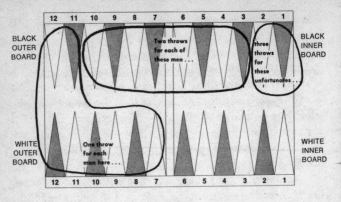

DIAGRAM 60

If you want a bit more sophistication and accuracy than this, you can break it down into half throws. It is the same principle: since the average movement of each throw is eight points, you count a half throw for each four-point span.

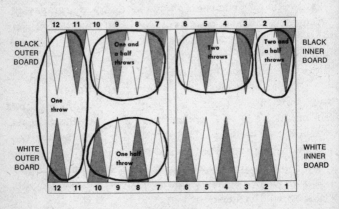

DIAGRAM 61

Either one of these methods should be memorized; it will be of value throughout the game. Personally, I prefer the second method. It is as fast to count, and since it blocks neatly into the board it is easier to visualize and remember.

As the game progresses and takes on its own momentum, there are five relationships that can develop:

(1) Your position is substantially ahead.
(2) You are only slightly ahead.
(3) You and your opponent are about equal.
(4) You are slightly behind.
(5) You are substantially behind.

Let's discuss your tactics for each of these.

You are substantially ahead. By this I mean that, roughly, you are at least a third or more ahead of your opponent: for every three throws necessary for you to get into your inner board, he needs the same *plus* one more. Specifically, he needs four throws for your three, eight for your six, etc. You can determine your own formula if you are not happy with this one; the principle, however, is the same.

Let's examine this situation in Diagram 62 on page 104.

Here, your count is a half throw for the man on the W9, and one throw each for the four men on B11 and B12—a total of four and a half throws to get in to your inner board. Black needs a half throw for each of his six men on the B7, B8, and B9 points; one throw for each of the three men on the W12 point, and one and a half throws for the man on the W10 point—a total of seven and a half throws to get in. If this is the case, you should consider doubling, of which more later. But if you don't (or can't, because the cube is in his posses-

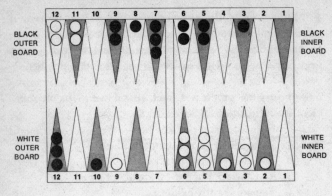

DIAGRAM 62

sion) and you play out this game, it would be wise to be even more cautious in leaving blots than you have been, as you obviously don't want to be slowed down at all. Move to points of safety when you can, making the best mileage possible. If you have to leave a blot, remember the ways in which it can be hit and try to place your man in the position of least danger. Don't take risks; you want to maintain your advantage. And your big concern should be to avoid helping your opponent go into a back game, which is exactly what he should do under these circumstances. We'll come to what a back game involves in just a moment.

The next three categories are obviously very similar, especially if it is still early in the game. Being a little ahead can easily change by virtue of a couple of bad rolls for you and a few good ones for your opponent; here you do not want to make too quick a decision. Therefore, if you are either slightly ahead or about even with your opponent, I would recommend the same tactics of safe moves I suggest when you are substantially ahead.

However, if your opponent is slightly ahead, you have another option. You can continue to play it cautiously for another throw or two, and see what develops, or you can open up. This situation usually arises at a time when both you and your opponent have covered several points in the outer boards in such a way that each of you is waiting for the other to open up one of them, hoping to get a shot at the other and slow him up, perhaps fatally. Such a board might look like Diagram 63:

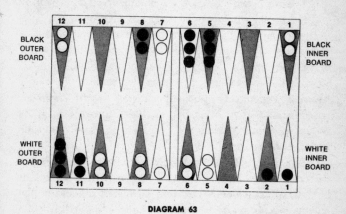

DIAGRAM 63

Here, White needs twelve and a half throws to get into his inner board: a half throw for each of the five men on the W7, W8, and W10 points; one throw each for the two men on the B12 point; one and a half throws for each of the two men on the B7 point; and two and a half throws for each of the two men on the B1 point. Black is only slightly ahead: he needs eleven throws to get in. It will probably take him one half throw for each of the two men on the B8 point; one throw for each of the five men on the W11 and W12 points;

and two and a half throws for each of the men on the W1 and W2 points.

Even though he is slightly behind in the count, the cautious player in White's situation, hoping he can hold out longer than his opponent, sits and waits like a cat for the mouse. The moves he makes while waiting are usually lower down, from his outer to his inner board; this is one reason for my earlier advice to retain that flexibility. Should you play it this way, this is the time to make some of the doors in the inner board so that a large number of them will be covered if and when your opponent is hit. Again, for flexibility, and also in the attempt to make a side prime before converting it into a prime, make the higher-numbered points first if you can. And, when you are building these doors, be careful: don't ever leave two blots at a time in your inner board. If you do, your opponent can open up with impunity; you are in a very vulnerable position. Conversely, if he should leave two blots on his inner board, it is an ideal time for you to open up.

But there is no certainty that he will have to open up first, and in such a case, especially since you are somewhat behind, you may decide to take a calculated risk and be the one to open up. Which is what I do: I flirt with the dice.

The necessary ingredient for this gamble is to have at least one door covered in your opponent's inner board. This safety point is your reservoir of strength. Having a lone blot on his inner board instead of a covered point is usually fatal. You will often find this hit as well and you may then be easily gammoned. But a covered point *and* a blot can be very strong; this is the perfect time to open up and take the chance.

So, being slightly behind and also able to go into a back game if I have to, I can at this moment risk virtually anything. If I now get a roll that involves taking a chance but promises to improve my position if it works, I play it that way. The timing is important: in effect, my opponent is damned if I'm hit and damned if I'm not. If the move works and I am not hit, I should be in a fairly good forward position; certainly in a better one than I was. And if it doesn't work and I am hit, I am perfectly willing and prepared to go into a back game. Either way, I should have the possibility of a good game. If it looks as though I may be the one who has to open up, I want to do so while there are still two or three points available in his inner board for me to come in on; remember how sharply the possibilities drop after four points are covered.

What to do if he opens up first? If he has only one or two men in your inner board, there's no question: hit him. But if he has three men back which are spread on two points, I would be very cautious and probably not hit the man he has just opened up as there is a danger in putting another man of his on the bar. This can give him a strong back game; rather than hit him again under these circumstances, I would wait another throw or two and see what develops, although I might hit the blot in my inner board if I have a sufficient number of points covered.

Hitting him in my inner board might slow him up without giving him a good opportunity for a strong back game; however, I do this only if his inner board is such that should he hit my resultant blot in turn, I won't be slowed up too much.

Finally, we come to the situation where you are substantially behind your opponent, that is where you need at least four throws to every three of his to get into your respective inner boards. Here, you are certain to lose if the dice continue as they have been going, so you have no choice: you must go into the back game immediately.

There are two elements necessary for a good back game. The first is to have two points covered in your opponent's inner board. These men are your ambush, and they are also islands of safety for you if you should have to bring in other men that your opponent may subsequently hit. With two points covered, you should have an excellent chance of getting a shot at one of his blots. Therefore, if you do not have this position when you decide to go into the back game, you should open up wherever practical around the board. Since having only two or three of your men in his back board are far less effective than four, you really have to try to get four men back and cover two points. Spread out your men as much as possible in an attempt either to entice him or force him to hit you. Remember the probabilities, and try to place these blots where they will be hardest for him to avoid. But try not to disturb your blocking points, especially in your side prime area, and certainly don't touch your men in his inner board unless you have three men on one point, in which case you should move one to another point if you can.

The question always arises: which points are the best to hold in your opponent's inner board? The assumption in the query is that you have some measure of control over which points you obtain. Unfortunately, you generally have very little choice. When possible, however, the points I like best are the 1 and the 3. Next is the 1 and 2 combination. Third choice is the 2 and 3. From there on it's really a toss-up.

The 1 and 3 is stronger than the 1 and 2 because when your opponent gets his men down to the lower points on his outer board, there are more chances of his being prevented from making a six or a five move if you are on the 1 and 2 rather than the 1 and 3. Since this is the critical time, when you want to hit him, it is wiser for you to give him every opportunity to leave a blot. You do this when you leave him the 2 point to land on. As for your holding the higher points in his inner board, I feel that they give you even less chance of getting a shot at your opponent's blot. For example, if you hold the 1 and 5 points, which some people like, you do put some pressure on him while he is moving into his outer board. However, because it is still relatively early, your blocking position is probably not that good yet, and so if you hit him now you are probably dissipating your strength rather than utilizing it. If instead you are covering points lower down in his inner board, chances are that you can hit him later in the game, when you have been able to close up your board more effectively.

This is the second element of a good back game: pacing. It is the manner in which you play your board while waiting to get that shot at your opponent. Now, the ideal board with which to win a back game is one on which you have made a prime, your remaining three men are not bottled up by your opponent, and he has one or two men on the bar. Not only is it ideal, it's doubling time. This is what you try to pace yourself to achieve; your movements while waiting to hit him should be consistent with this end purpose.

Consequently, if you see that you will probably have to wait a few throws before getting your shot at your opponent, and assuming you already have a fairly strong board built on your lower points, you should try to open up some of your other men and position them where they hopefully can get hit, so that you will be slowed down and therefore not have to break up your strength. This takes courage, for it can lead to a loss of a gammon, but it is the best way to make the back game work under these circumstances. I think it's worth the try. If your blocking position is not strong, and your men are fairly well spread out, then you need not try to be slowed down; instead, try to build your blocking points as much as possible. If you are in doubt, I suggest you try to get hit and be slowed down, but only if you have been able to maintain the two covered points in your opponent's inner board. There is less danger in being spread out and having men around the board with which you may be able to continue to hit him once you have sent him to the bar, than in allowing your board to break up too badly and no longer being able to block his progress. Remember, one of the hardest problems to face in playing a back game is to maintain your courage. This can be vital. Once you have gone into a back game, hang in there—until you hit, and the tide begins to turn.

Of course, the tide may not turn. You may not hit him, and your back game won't work. Don't hate me; it happens to me, too. If your opponent is worthy of your play, he is probably equally sophisticated in the elements of a back game and understandably will be loath to cooperate. He may even have read this book . . . At any rate, there may come a time when you should run like hell to avoid a gammon or, adding insult to injury, the backgammon. This is something I will discuss in the chapter on bearing off. For now, let's assume your back game is working, and you not only get an opportunity to hit, but do.

Once you have hit him, the way you play depends on the relative positions on the board. There are now two possibilities: first, where he is still potentially ahead of you; and second, where the situation has now reversed, and you are potentially ahead of him.

If he can get back in and around easily, and is still ahead of you in the number of throws necessary to get off, then you must slow him down further. You have to utilize your men that are not on important blocking points and spread them

out as much as posssible in an attempt to hit him again and
again as he comes around; for this you need as many possibilities as you can manage. Stay out of his range; try to
maneuver so that you don't leave blots within six points of
his man prior to his throw or he may hit you and turn the
tables. But if it is a choice, that is, even if hitting him means
you'll leave a potentially vulnerable blot, you still should
do it. It's a chance you must take, for you must slow him
down—or lose. Bear in mind the number of ways a blot can
be hit on the various points; constantly apply this knowledge. And now you also want to make as quickly as possible
either your prime (preferable, especially if he is still on the
bar) or side prime. To do this, you need to bring some of
your men down to your inner and outer boards so that you
have enough men with which to build these points. So, while
you are moving down and trying to get a prime made, open
up your men on his outer board, and also your back men.
You no longer want to have points made in his back board,
because two men on two points instead of both on one point
more than double your possibilities of hitting him as he
comes around. Keep these men in his inner board until last;
they are sometimes your final hope. A lucky throw may get
his man past most of your scattered waiting men; you then
have only this last chance of hitting him. Have the courage to
stay back and wait with one or two of your men; a gammon
is never that likely in this situation.

But keep counting throws to determine your relative
positions: the balance now is probably very delicate, and you
have to watch for the moment when you have become more
advanced than he. Whenever this happens—that is, when
you are potentially ahead of him in the number of throws
necessary to win—you have achieved the aim of the back
game; you now have to shift your tactics into those of the

running game. At this point, you must exercise extreme caution, while getting the best value you can from your throws. Try not to give him the chance to hit you if you can avoid it; if you can't, then remember the probabilities and give him the least likely shot you can. But if you play carefully, you should now have the game won.

Now let's talk about the reverse situation.

Earlier, in discussing the situation where you were substantially ahead, I pointed out that you should avoid helping your opponent go into a back game. Now that I have elaborated on a good back game and the necessary elements for one, it should be easy for you to tell when it is your opponent who should be going into one and what he needs for it. Consequently, you now can anticipate his motives and not help him achieve these ends.

First, seriously consider throwing the doubling cube at him, if it is not already in his possession. Should you decide not to throw it, or if you do and he accepts it, then do not hit a fourth man of his if he already has three men in your inner board. Even if these men of his are not well-positioned, it is something to avoid. It suddenly can happen that you have several shots at him and you think you can win a gammon if you send another of his men to the bar; too often this turns out to be a cruel illusion.

Take this situation in Diagram 64 on page 113, for example:

Looking at it, it seems as though you have an excellent chance for a gammon: you need only four and a half throws to get in to your inner board, and your opponent—once he gets his man on the bar back on the board—needs at least twelve throws to get in. However, he is in a very good position to go into a back game, especially if you should be put in a position where you cannot avoid hitting him again, and

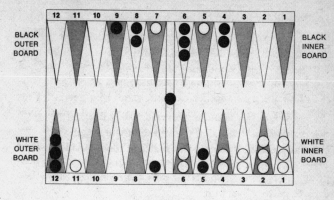

DIAGRAM 64

so I say throw the cube and get it over with if you think he will refuse it. Beware of that greed which may lead you to take dangerous chances by going for the gammon.

When you are playing against the possibility of your opponent's going into a back game, it is also wise to get any of your men remaining in his inner board out of there as soon as possible. At this stage you no longer should be maintaining the option of going into a back game. And you cannot take the chance that these men will get trapped back there and consequently force you to break up the blocking strength you have developed on your lower outer board and your inner board.

In addition, try to hamper your opponent's mobility. I do not mean you should hit him, for that is the prime precaution: don't let him get four men back in your inner board. But I do mean that if he has two or three men in your inner board, then at least while you are consolidating your position and bringing your men around and into your inner board, you should try to keep his men from escaping. This will force him to break up his own board and open the way, should he later hit you, for you to easily get back in and around. And if you have this capability, it of course effectively destroys any hope he may still retain for a back game.

This leads to another caution: should he get all of his men, other than those in your inner board, piled up on his 1, 2, or 3 points, he will have what is known as a speedboard—that is, one from which he can quickly bear off once he starts doing so, for with it he is virtually certain of taking two men off on every throw. No matter how often he may throw low dice, they can't hurt him.

When he has such a speedboard, you have to be careful, for he is now probably ahead of you in the number of throws necessary to bear off. Therefore a lucky roll—a double 5 or 6, say—which gets him out of your board and quickly around, may allow him to win suddenly. Therefore, even though he has some men in your inner board, you must keep counting; when it seems that this danger exists, you should try to hit him. In this situation you want to slow him down and protect yourself against the unlucky possibility of his throwing big dice. And you must do so even if it means taking a chance on being hit yourself. But remember: since he has a speedboard, you can re-enter easily should he hit you.

These, then, are the tactics for you to know as the game progresses. As you apply them, they will (hopefully) make for a more interesting, more enjoyable, and more profitable game.

There are several other tactical matters I'd like to discuss, points that do not necessarily relate to a specific position of the mid-game but apply generally throughout the course of play.

The B12 point is an extremely valuable one, a fortress of strength that should not be broken down unless there is no real alternative. As long as there is any possible use for it as an escape station, or to threaten enemy blots coming out of your inner board, keep it. I would usually rather take the chance of being hit somewhere else than breaking it up too soon; if you lose this point too early, trouble usually comes later.

Another point to be particularly careful of is the B7. It can be a strong point if you cover it early in the game, but it quickly becomes treacherous and should be vacated early. Otherwise, as the game progresses you will find it increasingly difficult to escape from it safely. I have found that a very good time to open up such a point is when I am in that middle position I described earlier, where I am trying to precipitate the decision as to the kind of game I shall play.

If the situation should arise where you have a man (or men) in your opponent's inner board and he has a side prime blocking them, don't hit him if he should leave a blot. This will only delay his breaking up this prime, and consequently also delay the escape of your men. In turn this would lead you to break up your own blocking strength. And even if your opponent has only five points of the side prime, I would caution the same behavior, especially if you have more than one man in his inner board. It can be very difficult to get them both out.

When you are entering a man from the bar and you can bring him in on either of two points, in general you should put him on the lower point of the two. This will prove valuable if your opponent should hit this blot again, for the lower down he moves his men, the more effectively they are out of action. In addition, should you go into a back game, it is the lower points that are of most value to you.

Try to position your builders as advantageously as

possible. Three points near each other with three men on each is far better than two points with four, so split your builders whenever possible. For example, look at Diagram 65.

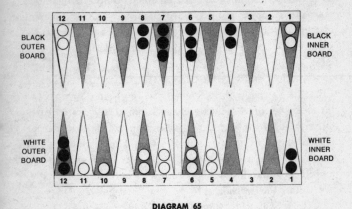

DIAGRAM 65

Let's assume you have thrown a 5 - 4. Some people would bring the two blots to the W6 point, on the theory that not only are they safe but that two more men are in the inner board. However, the better move is to bring the man from the W10 to the W5, and the man from the W11 to the W7. The reason is simple: having five men on the W6 point is of value to close another point only if you get double 1, 2, 3, or 4; having the builders on the 5, 6, and 7 points allows you to make a point with a 1 - 1, 2 - 2, 1 - 3, 3 - 1, 2 - 3, 3 - 2, 1 - 2, 2 - 1, 3 - 4, 4 - 3, 2 - 4, 4 - 2, 4 - 5, 5 - 4, 3 - 5, or 5 - 3. Thus, by moving the first way (both to the W6) there are only four throws that can utilize these men; the second way gives you sixteen possibilities. So, whenever you can, spread your men for building purposes rather than piling them up on a single point.

Finally, an important admonition: be comfortable. I'm talking about a lot of little things, but small matters can easily become big annoyances and result in losses because of a lack of concentration. I'm talking about playing on a board of a decent size. I'm talking about the ambiance: the lighting, the noise, the chairs, the height of the table, the feel of the crowd. Then there's the matter of pace: play at your own, not too hurried, not too slow. (If your opponent starts to rush you, when you've been reasonable, slow down some more: you'll be amazed at how much this will rattle him!) I also suggest you not get *too* comfortable: don't drink that much; it's lethal. And, of course, the biggest comfort: when you win, collect!

8. THE PREGNANT BACK BOARD: THE ODDS OF BEARING OFF

In talking of bearing off, I like to think of the back board as pregnant and ready to bring forth. Unfortunately, some pregnancies miscarry.

Basically, there are two situations that occur at this stage of the game. First, your opponent still has men either in your inner board or on the bar and has the possibility of hitting you. Second, there is no longer any contact with him and it is a straight race.

This latter situation is the easier one, because it is mainly mechanical. Every move must be utilized to its utmost; not a point can be wasted. Your first objective is to get all your men into your inner board as fast as possible. Therefore, it is your 6 point that you should aim for. Even if this makes you very heavy on this point, you may be able to begin bearing off one or two throws earlier than if you didn't use this tactic. And there is always the possibility of a double 6 throw, which would lighten your load considerably.

High throws of the dice should not be used to move men from your outer board on to lower points in your inner board if you still have any men further away, such as on your opponent's outer board. Those men which are further away should first be brought down to your outer board, so that they can be brought in from there to your inner board with the throw on one die.

As you move into your inner board, try to place your men on points that are open if this does not waste part of your move, as this will help you at least intially to bear off one man for each die you throw. The same principle applies once you start bearing off; if you cannot take a man off with the move, then if possible use it to cover open points rather than piling up men on any one point.

There's a magic number to remember, for it can help you in positioning your men, especially toward the end when you have only two men left. This number is 2 - 5, and it is magical because it represents a probable winning combination for you. Look at the board in Diagram 66, on page 120.

Let's assume you throw a 6 - 2. You bear off one man from your 5 point and then you must move the 2. Most players I've seen, when in a situation like this, would move from the higher point: that is, they would move the man remaining on W5 to W3. Since Black will certainly remove two of his men on his next throw (assuming he doesn't throw doubles) and then will bear off his last two men on his next throw, you can win only by getting both your men off on

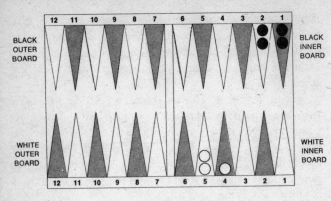

DIAGRAM 66

your next throw. So, the question here is whether you made the best move possible for your 6 - 2 throw. The answer is no.

You had no choice about bearing off one of the men on W5 for the 6 move, but instead of moving the other W5 man to W3, leaving you with men on the 3 and 4 points, you should have moved the man on W4 to W2, leaving you with men on the 2 and 5 points. This is because with a 2 and 5 position you have *more* than a 50-50 chance to get both men off in one throw. Any position better than this will simply be that much surer of winning, and any position worse than this brings your chance of winning below the 50-50 mark. And that is why 2 - 5 is the magical number.

The 2 - 5 combination is crucial for this purpose, and you cannot trifle with it. That is, you cannot think that a 1 - 6 or a 3 - 4 are as good because they also total 7—which is the way some people count: by totals. Here, the total is not critical, but the fact that one man *must* be on the 2 point (or better), and the other man *must* be on the 5 point (or better), if you want to have at least a 50 percent chance to bear off in one throw.

For purists, here are the facts: with a 2 and 5 position, you can get off in nineteen ways out of the thirty-six possible throws of the dice: 2 - 2, 3 - 3, 4 - 4, 5 - 5, 6 - 6, 2 - 5, 5 - 2, 2 - 6, 6 - 2, 3 - 5, 5 - 3, 3 - 6, 6 - 3, 4 - 5, 5 - 4, 4 - 6, 6 - 4, 5 - 6, 6 - 5. Men on the 3 and 4 points cut your chances to seventeen ways: 2 - 2, 3 - 3, 4 - 4, 5 - 5, 6 - 6, 3 - 4, 4 - 3, 3 - 5, 5 - 3, 3 - 6, 6 - 3, 4 - 5, 5 - 4, 4 - 6, 6 - 4, 5 - 6, 6 - 5. And if you have men on the 1 and 6 points, you can win with only fifteen of the thirty-six throws: 2 - 2, 3 - 3, 4 - 4, 5 - 5, 6 - 6, 1 - 6, 6 - 1, 2 - 6, 6 - 2, 3 - 6, 6 - 3, 4 - 6, 6 - 4, 5 - 6, and 6 - 5.

Consequently, and especially in a close race, when it is getting down to the wire, 2 - 5 is what you should aim for.

Should you have a slightly better position than this, remember that the 5 is more sensitive than the 2. That is, move the man from the 2 point to the 1 point before moving the man on the 5 point to the 4 point. Although there are the same number of ways to bear off a 1 - 5 position and a 2 - 4 position (twenty-three), you are considerably better with a 1 - 4 position (twenty-nine ways) than with a 2 - 3 position (twenty-five ways).

And for a position that is slightly worse than the 2 - 5, the rule is the same: play with the two before you disturb the five. For example, you are better with a 3 - 5 position (fourteen ways) than a 2 - 6 position (thirteen ways).

Also, it is most important to remember that if you have a choice in making your moves in your inner board, it is vastly preferable to have a man alone on a higher point than to have two men split on the lower points, even if the total number of points necessary to bear off is the same. Let's take as an example Diagram 67 on page 122.

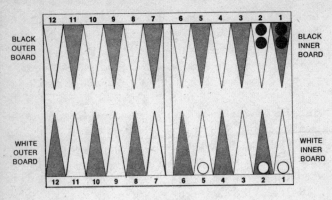

DIAGRAM 67

Assume you now get a 2 - 1 throw. You can play it in three ways and not leave an odd third man:

(1) Bear off the man from the 1 point and move the man on the 5 point to the 3 point, leaving a 2 - 3 position.

(2) Bear off the man from the 2 point, and move the man on the 5 point to the 4 point, leaving a 1 - 4 position.

(3) Bear off the men from both the 1 and the 2 points, leaving only the man on the 5 point.

As I pointed out above, the 2 - 3 position can be borne off in one throw in only twenty-five ways. The 1 - 4 position —remember, it's the man on the 1 point that makes it better— is good in twenty-nine ways. But the man alone on the 5 is a tower of strength: he can get off in thirty-one ways. And this principle of leaving a single man on a higher point in preference to two men on lower points is consistently valid, no matter what the total number of points needed to bear off may be.

As another example, let's look at Diagram 68:

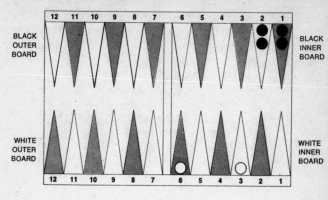

DIAGRAM 68

Again assume a 2 - 1 throw. Do you take off the man from the 3 point, or do you move the man from the 6 point to the 3 point, so that you have two men on it? The two men together can get off in only seventeen ways, whereas the man alone on the 6 can make it in twenty-seven ways! (Don't confuse this with the number of ways to hit a blot—here you are good with every throw totaling more than a six as well.) Clearly, doubling up your men is not the way to do it. Finally, compare these with the chances for the 1 - 5 or 2 - 4 positions, both of which are good in twenty-three ways.

Thus the rule—which applies to all the situations that can occur in that last moment of bearing off—is if you have a choice, better to leave a single man on a higher point than have two men split lower down; and either of these positions is preferable to having two men together on a point.

All these rules for bearing off have an added value: while you are still bringing your men in to your inner board, your last few men in your outer board should be positioned in accordance with these suggestions for bearing off. Practically, you aim for the 6 point on your inner board just the way you try to place your men on your inner board when you are bearing off.

For example:

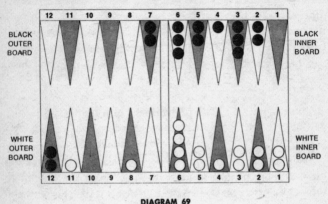

DIAGRAM 69

As you can see, for the purpose of getting into your inner board, the W8 and W11 points are in effect the same as the W2 and W5 points for the purpose of bearing off. Thus the rules for placement of men in the outer board are the same as for the inner board.

Now let's get to the other situation, where your opponent still has men either in your inner board or on the bar, and has the possibility of hitting you. You know that he is lurking in ambush, waiting for an opportunity to rob you of the game that should rightfully be yours. But, as opposed to the old Western stagecoach dramas, you not only know he is there waiting for you, but you also know where he is and how strong he is. That's a big advantage.

You need this advantage, for the situation can be a complicated one. If you want to know how complicated, here's one fact that will illustrate it well: if your opponent has two points covered in your inner board, there are 1,820 *different* ways in which you can place your fifteen men on the remaining four points. And if he has only one point covered, you have 4,368 combinations possible!

Let's go into some principles that will help in this placement.

As you bring your men into your inner board, you should always keep in mind the probabilities of a blot being hit if you have to leave one. If so, leave it where it is least likely to be hit. Don't make it easy for your opponent.

You must avoid having an odd number of men on your highest two points. By this I mean that if you have men on the 5 and 6 points, with two men on your 5 point, you should have two men or four men on your 6 point, *not* three men. And if you have three men on your 5 point, you should have three men on your 6 point. These last two points should always have an equal number of men, or an even number of men. If they do not, you can find yourself in trouble on your next throw about twice as often.

Once you start bearing off, never leave three men on the highest point you still hold. For example, if you have cleared your 6 point and your 5 point, and now the highest point you hold is the 4 point, having three men on it can kill you, for you can be hurt by any throw containing two high dice. So be very careful: if you can, keep two men or four men on that last point.

As you bear off men, in general try to do so from the highest point you have covered; keep your lower board solid against him as long as you can. But there is an important exception to this: if breaking your highest point will leave three men on the next highest point, instead of two or four men on it, then move within the board (or bear off) from a lower point if you can. Look at this situation and assume you throw a 5 - 1. What would you say is the best way to play it?

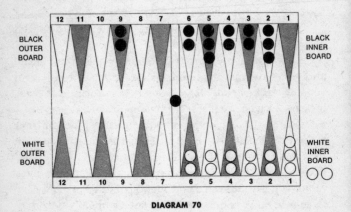

DIAGRAM 70

The general rule would have you break from the 6 point, moving one man to your 1 point and one man to your 5 point. But this would leave you with three men on your 5 point as in Diagram 71 on page 127.

Now, if Black does not get in on his next throw, there are seventeen ways you can be in danger on your next roll by having to leave a blot (2 - 5, 5 - 2, 3 - 5, 5 - 3, 4 - 5, 5 - 4, 2 - 6, 6 - 2, 3 - 6, 6 - 3, 4 - 6, 6 - 4, 5 - 6, 6 - 5, 4 - 4, 5 - 5, and 6 - 6).

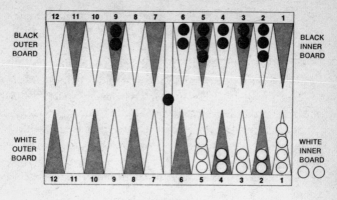

DIAGRAM 71

However, if you instead were to break your 5 point, you would have this board:

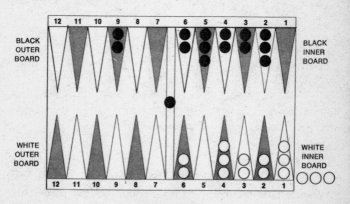

DIAGRAM 72

Again, assuming Black does not get in on his next throw, you can then be in trouble only with a 1 - 5, 5 - 1, 1 - 6, 6 - 1, 4 - 4, 5 - 5, or 6 - 6—only seven ways.

Thus you can see that a third man on your highest point, other than the 6 point, can be a danger and is to be avoided. And don't forget that if you have three men on your 6 point, you better have three men on your 5 point too.

Remember that you are not required to make the higher move first: you can move the lower one first if you wish. I have seen good players forget this in the heat of battle; it's an easy mistake. Just to fix it firmly in mind, let's take this board:

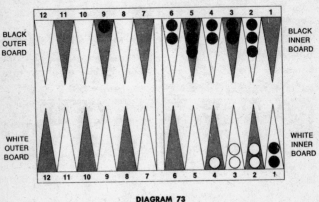

DIAGRAM 73

Here, assume you throw a 4 - 1. The correct play is to make the one move first, from the 4 point to the 3 point, and then to bear this man off. It's obvious, but sometimes too obvious. Unfortunately, some over-anxious players take off the man from the 4 point, and then move a man from W3 to W2, leaving a vulnerable blot on W3. A simple mistake. . . .

If your opponent should leave a blot in your inner board, you may be very tempted to hit it. This can be a delicate matter, and you have to weigh several factors. If you can hit him and cover your man (either by making the point or moving this man on to a point you already have made), so you do not leave a blot open for your opponent to get a shot at, and you also are able to avoid the dangers I've talked about above, then maybe you should hit him.

You should not hit him if he has a fairly strong position against you in his inner board, or is close to a side prime, for your hitting him will consequently slow down his having to break up his board. But if you don't hit him, either he will have to run this man in your inner board and remove him from being a threat against you, or he will have to break up his board, or both.

You also should not hit him unless it will do you some benefit. If you are already substantially ahead of him, yet you are not really in a good enough position to expect a gammon, then why hit him? In this case you should let him get past your men if possible, so that he is no longer a threat; if he is on the bar, he can be a real danger. Of course, if you are *not* enough ahead of your opponent in the number of throws necessary to get off, so that a lucky throw could suddenly put him ahead of you, then you have to hit him to hassle him and make him lose time.

Also, if he should leave two blots in your inner board, try to hit them both if his inner board is fairly open. Then if he hits you in turn you can easily get back in and around. Should he not hit you, and you can cover or bear off these blots, you will then be in a good position to win a gammon. However, when he leaves two blots, it is usually wise not to hit just one of them unless there is a strong advantage, such as the need to slow him down. This is because if you hit one of these two blots, and he then comes back in on the other one, this point he has just made in your inner board can make your life very difficult.

So, don't hit his blot in your inner board unless: (a) he is in a position where a lucky throw can put him ahead of you in the race to bear off, and so you have to hassle him; or (b) there is a good chance of winning a gammon because of it.

If you should have to leave a blot in your inner board, remember that if all the intervening points between your opponent's point and your blot are covered by you, then there are exactly eleven ways for him to hit you, no matter what the distance. A blot on your 6 point is as vulnerable as a blot on your 3 point, if in both cases all the intervening points are covered by you.

This can be important when you have a choice on where to leave a blot: a situation may arise where you can move a man down and leave a blot on a higher point, or bear off a man on a lower point and leave a blot there. Since there is no difference in the number of ways in which either blot can be hit, it is of value to leave it on the lower point and bear off a man as well. Should you be hit and therefore delayed, every additional man off the board may be crucial.

Now let's discuss the situation when *you* are playing the back game. Since this is detailed in the strategy chapter, there is only one matter to go into here: how best to avoid a gammon (or even worse: a backgammon) if your back game isn't working.

It really is that simple: when a back game doesn't make it, a gammon can easily result. Therefore, you have to weigh your chances of winning as opposed to the chances of a gammon.

The first part of this question—how much chance of

winning do you have?—is the hardest part, so let's hold it for a moment. The second part—what is the chance of a gammon?—is easier. Since a back game that doesn't work can frequently result in a gammon, it really is a matter of determining *when* you can expect to be gammoned if you stay in the back game and don't succeed. Up to this moment you can be fairly sure that if you choose to run you can avoid a gammon; past this point you can be just as sure that you've had it if you don't hit him. And determining this moment of truth when the balance tips against you is relatively easy.

You will recall from our counting system that one of your men in your opponent's inner board, on the B1 or B2 points, probably needs two and a half throws to get in to your inner board; two men there will consequently require five throws. Since it takes an extra throw to bear a man off, you will probably need a total of six throws to avoid a gammon if you are holding only the B1 point. Of course, if any of your other men should not be in your inner board, you must also count the appropriate number of throws for them.

As for your opponent, for practical purposes in this situation you can count one and a half throws for each two men still remaining for him to bear off. He may need less for men on his lower points, and he may need more for men on the higher ones, but this is a realistic and conservative average which allows for the possibility of cautious moves on his part.

Therefore, if you have two men on his 1 point and need six throws to bear off, you will be in a position of balance with him when he has eight men left to bear off, as he will probably require six throws as well. And it follows in this instance that when your opponent has anything less than eight men left to be borne off you are in danger of being gammoned (at least) if you do not hit him.

Of course, your board may be wide open, with men spread all around, when he starts bearing off, so the count would show that the balance has already gone against you. Here's an example:

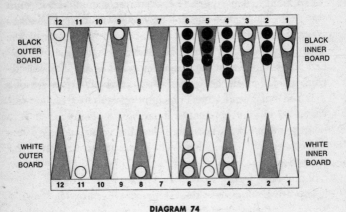

DIAGRAM 74

Counting, you will find that you need thirteen throws to get all your men into your inner board: two and a half for each of the two men on B1, two throws for each of the two men on B3, one and a half for the man on B9, one each for the men on B12 and W11, and one half throw for the man on W8. You then also need another throw to bear off a man, so you have to figure on a probable fourteen throws to avoid a gammon. Your opponent, however, is already ahead of you, for he should be able to get off in twelve throws. Even so, it is fairly close, and if you were to get a couple of lucky throws, you might be able to avoid a gammon if you were to run now.

However, because you are in a very good position to play

a strong back game, with an excellent chance to win, it would be criminal to even think of trying to run at this moment.

And there's the answer to the first question I posed a while back: when your board is that good for a strong back game so that you probably can win once you get the shot you're waiting for, you stay in the back game even at the risk of a gammon. It's worth the chance.

Should your board not be as good, in terms of the requirements of the back game, you obviously have less of a chance to win, and so you must give serious thought to what you are doing back there. Although it is always possible to win, even with a bad board and most of your opponent's men off, let's be realistic: it may be wiser to take the loss and avoid the gammon. Learn from the loss if you can; try to analyze the situation to see if you made a mistake and, if so, what it was. I do not mean to imply that you did make a mistake. The dice may have given you no opportunities; nor, presumably, is your opponent inept. I know that I never make mistakes, yet I lose gammons. . . .

However, you should not lose a *backgammon:* that's too much of an indignity. Here are some thoughts on saving face.

By the time your opponent has reached the point of having only a few men left to bear off, you should have all of your men in your inner board, with the exception of those men still in his inner board. As a general rule you should never have more than two men on any point in your opponent's inner board; additional men are never of any value and merely increase the risk of a double or triple game. But here the question arises: when is it wiser to have only *one* man on a point?

There are a few considerations in this matter. First, in

terms of gammons and backgammons, is that the fewer men you have in your opponent's inner board, the less chance there is of a double or triple game. Second, in certain situations, by having a single man on a point instead of covering it, you do not block a move that your opponent would otherwise be able to avoid, and which might be your last hope to hit him. For example, take this board, and assume he throws anything that has a 1 on one of the dice—2 - 1, 3 - 1, 4 - 1, 5 - 1, or 6 - 1:

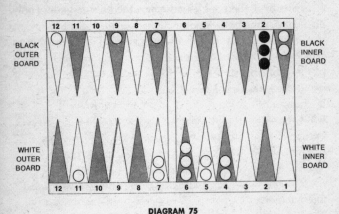

DIAGRAM 75

If you have two men on B1, then he will not be able to make the move for the die showing 1, and so he will bear off only one man, keeping his last two men protected. But if you have only one man on the B1 point, he will then have to bear off one man and hit you for the 1 move, thereby giving your blot two shots at him.

If you leave a blot on B1, instead of keeping two men there, it helps accomplish the first purpose as well. Should this blot be the only man left in your opponent's inner board at the time he is hit, then you no longer can be back-gammoned, for in this situation any throw of the dice will allow you to get back on the board and either hit one of the two Black blots or get you out of his inner board.

In this instance, your leaving a blot, as opposed to keep-ing the point covered, is the wise move.

Should your blot not be hit and your opponent manages to bear off two men, you will now have thirty-four ways in which to hit his blot on B2 or escape the backgammon (only a 3 - 2 throw prevents this).

The same basic considerations hold true when you are covering two points:

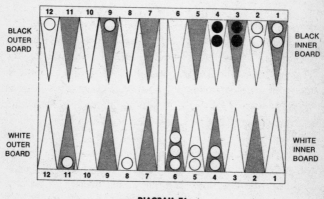

DIAGRAM 76

Let's assume your throw will allow you to move a man from either of the two points you are covering. If you do so from the B2 point, leaving a blot there, eight of your op-ponent's throws force him to leave two blots, and ten other throws force him to leave one blot. (I'm not concerned that on some of these moves he can hit you: having a man on the bar is really not much worse, in terms of a gammon or back-gammon, than a man on the B1 or B2 points. I'm concerned about the best way you can get a shot at him.)

If you move one of your men from the B1 point, leaving a blot there, there are six throws in which he is forced to leave three blots (2 - 4, 4 - 2, 2 - 5, 5 - 2, 2 - 6, and 6 - 2) and twelve more ways (1 - 2, 2 - 1, 1 - 3, 3 - 1, 2 - 3, 3 - 2, 3 - 4, 4 - 3, 3 - 5, 5 - 3, 3 - 6, and 6 - 3) in which he must leave one blot. If you don't open up either of these points, but make your move elsewhere on the board, six of his throws will force him to leave two blots, and twelve of them will force him to leave one blot.

Therefore, opening up the B1 point gives you the most shots at your opponent, and so is the move to make. I find this particularly interesting, because most players I've watched in this situation would instinctively break up the B2 point before the B1. Breaking up the B1 point, as opposed to keeping both points intact, has one additional advantage: there is now one less man in your opponent's inner board, which considerably helps your chances of avoiding a back-gammon.

Finally, there is one small formula you can use when you are down to holding one point in your opponent's inner board and he has more than one point covered. If his men on these points total an even number, don't leave a blot. If his men total an odd number, *do* leave a blot. There are pages of diagrams to illustrate this, but it's too laborious to go into. Just believe me: keep the total of all men (yours and his) that are in his inner board an even number. It's your best hope.

9. THE DIABOLICAL DOUBLER: BETTING FOR BLOOD

There is nothing quite so evil as the smile on a player's face when he throws the doubling cube at his opponent. Except the cube itself.

But the cube is more: it is also a lethal weapon, and it should be used as such. To be specific, it can often achieve its goal by threatening or bluffing the victim into submission.

If you're not too familar with the cube, read about it first in Chapter Two, where it is described in basic detail. Here, it's strictly big business. Very simply, the cube is designed to persuade your opponent of the righteousness of your cause, which is to make money. Help with this purpose is what I'll try to give you here. Successful use of the doubling cube serves several other purposes in addition to the basic desire of winning money: it foregoes the necessity of playing out a probably dull game, and, more importantly, it also precludes both possibilities of his getting fantastically good dice or your getting fantastically bad ones, either resulting in the unfortunate situation of losing the game.

It is this possibility of losing the game you have unhappily doubled that brings us to a fascinating absurdity of the cube, which I'd like to point out here, for it affects your decision in whether or not to accept the cube. Simply put (and for the moment not considering gammons or backgammons), the cube doubles the net game for the one using it but, in effect, *triples* the potential winnings for the opponent who accepts it.

It is apparent that the person throwing the cube can win or lose two dollars if the game is played out, rather than the initial stake of one dollar (which is what we'll assume the basic bet to be to illustrate this discussion). He has merely doubled the bet and the amount that he can win or lose.

Paradoxically, however, the player who accepts the cube is not similarly doubling his bet. For him, it is different —and better.

Since you have no choice about the cube's being thrown at you, when it is you then have only the two options open: either pay the dollar or gamble another dollar on the chance of winning. That is, give up, and pay one; play on, and you may have to pay two. Therefore, at this point your actual gamble is *only one dollar*, because you have no choice about the first dollar: it must be paid in either event. However, for this gamble of an additional dollar, should you win you not only collect the two-dollar stake from your opponent, but you also save the dollar you otherwise would have paid—a net gain to you, therefore, of three dollars. So, by accepting the cube, you are accepting odds of 3 to 1, a much more advantageous take than the seemingly obvious—but incorrect—odds of 2 to 1. These odds of 3 to 1, incidentally, apply no matter what number the cube is on when it is thrown. This is not sophistry; it is simple mathematics.

If you accepted the cube and were then gammoned, don't fret. It happens to all of us. But if it happens to you often, you probably should more carefully examine your practice of accepting doubles. Maybe you're being foolhardy, confusing it with bravery; maybe you're not analyzing your position accurately enough. As for the odds involved: if you accepted the cube, lost a gammon, and now have to pay four dollars, you actually lost an equal-odds bet. That is, if you had not accepted the cube, you would have lost—and paid—one dollar. So, you actually lost three more, and since you had the opportunity of winning at least a net of three dollars (assuming you did not gammon your opponent), the real odds for you were 3 to 3, or even. If you were *back*gammoned, it was a 5 to 3 gamble.

The elementary rule of the cube is to use it only if and when you have a distinct advantage over your opponent. By this I mean that your game must be sufficiently strong so that, unless your opponent suddenly gets fantastic dice, you are at least reasonably sure of beating him. I do not say "a *very* good chance of beating him," for I want to make a distinction. It seems to me that if you have a very good chance of winning, you have a pretty good chance for a gammon. In this event, you may not want to throw the cube too soon; you may prefer to wait. If your game gets even stronger, fine. But if it should start to slacken off, you presumably are still in a strong enough position to throw the cube and force him out.

However, I happen to believe that in general one wins

when one can: that is, one dollar won is better than two that may be lost. Therefore, when I believe that my opponent will not accept the cube, I double. I don't want him to accept, ever. As far as I'm concerned, the cube is not a doubling tool; it is primarily a weapon with which I expect to force my opponent out of the game. I always want him to refuse, for I distrust and fear the fickleness of the dice. Therefore, I will usually take the game when I can and not be greedy, because greed—like any *hubris*—can be my downfall. In general, I do not throw the cube when I think he will accept it, unless I am quite confident of winning the game.

This leads to the matter of the behavior pattern of your opponent. Some people accept the cube almost invariably; against such a player I handle it in just that fashion. With him, I wait. I wait until I am virtually certain that I will win at least the game if not a gammon; *then* I throw the cube. If my opponent follows his pattern, he will accept, and then I will win double the bet at relatively no gamble. Should I gammon him, it's like strawberries in winter! Yet another advantage against such a player is that if my game suddenly goes sour before I throw the cube, I am saved the possible resulting embarrassment of losing a double game.

Other players crumble at the sight of the cube. They sit there, staring at the board, then at you, looking somewhat like a betrayed basset hound. Finally, the sigh and the capitulation. This is what is known as an easy mark, and you don't need any advice about playing against him. Just keep throwing the cube and collecting.

If your opponent is not one who crumbles too easily, however, but is a reasonably good player and appraiser of his situation, it is wise not to double too early. Even a strong advantage can quickly evaporate. Suddenly you're redoubled, and it's disaster time. Against such a player, I wait.

An apparent advantage early in the game is often only that: apparent. And a good player knows this, so he will usually—and especially if he also knows the 3 to 1 odds situation I talked about earlier—accept such a double. But if your strength remains, you can always double later in the game, when there is less time remaining for the vagaries of war to shift to his favor. Or, if your early strength turns to real power, you might then prefer not to double but instead go for the gammon.

This, then, is the first rule of the cube: don't double too early.

There are certain factors to look for before throwing the double when there is still contact between you. By "contact," I mean that it is a mid-game situation where you each have men to still get past some of the opponent's men; the matter of doubling once there is no longer any contact is treated later.

For a successful mid-game double, in essence not only must your position be further advanced than your opponent's to some discernible degree, but (as importantly) he should not have a good board for a back game. If this is the case, then throw the cube at him. If his evaluation of his own position is as bleak as yours, and if he has any brains, he probably will not take the double. Specifically, these are the factors I recommend you look for before throwing the cube:

(1) You should have two or three of his men—not four—bottled up in your inner board.

(2) You should have a strong blocking position of at least four or five points covered, preferably in sequence.

(3) You should not have more than one of your men in the comparable situation of being bottled up in his inner board.

(4) You should be further advanced than he is in your forward game by at least the value of two or three throws.

(5) Finally, and most importantly, your opponent should not be in a good position to go into a back game.

It is this last point that is vital: how strong are his chances in a back game? If the possibility exists that he can go into a good one, and especially if he is a sophisticated player who understands it, don't double! In this case, it would be wise to wait for another few throws and see what develops. Practically, this is the second rule of the cube: when you are further advanced than your opponent, and he no longer has a chance for a good back game, double.

The reverse also applies, of course, when the cube is thrown at you. Assuming the above factors are present for your opponent, and unless you feel fairly confident that you will be able to go into at least a respectable back game, you should not accept such a double. To do so is to invite disaster.

Indeed, I find that the hardest decision I ever have to make is not when to throw the cube, but rather when not to accept it. It's easy to throw it; it's easy to accept it. But is it hard to refuse! For me, as for most people, it's partly bravado, masquerading as bravery, especially if a pretty girl is watching. But it's probably even more the nature of the beast: if I was not a gambler, really enjoying the game and the excitement that a revolving cube may bring, I wouldn't be here. I tend to gamble all the way, which makes me an easy mark, at least in this regard. So are most players: we accept foolish doubles, hoping for—and somewhat expecting as our due—the miracle toss. But the unfortunate truth is that this toss just doesn't occur often enough. And, of course, it can happen for my opponent just as readily as it can for me; if it does, a gammon, doubled and accepted, can be a true disgrace.

The decision to accept the cube should be based on only one question: how good is your chance of winning? It should not—it *must* not—be based on any other factor. The amount the game is worth at that moment is immaterial; the amount that you are winning—or, especially, losing—at that moment is immaterial; the hour of the night is immaterial. All that should affect your decision is the probability of losing versus the possibility of winning. You cannot depend on lucky dice; you cannot—if you have been losing money—accept doubles in an attempt to win it back faster; you should not entertain the thought of making it a more exciting evening because it is beginning to draw to a close. Take the cool, hard-headed businessman's approach to the cube before throwing it or accepting it: what are the realistic chances of its making money for you?

I say "realistic chances," for every once in a while I, like you, take unrealistic ones. The probabilities dictate one course of action; I sometimes take the risk of the other. I'm a gambler, so I rationalize this by saying I heard the dice, or I just felt that I should, or some other such nonsense. If it pays off, I can play the big hero; more often, I'm the fool. But to win consistently, which is what this book is about, keep the risk element to a minimum and play the odds.

The biggest gulp is when the cube is already at eight or sixteen, say, and is thrown back at you. There is a tendency to accept it because you don't want to give up that big a game. Resist the tendency. The merits or non-merits of accepting the cube are not related to the size of the bet; if anything, the tendency should be in the other direction. It is far better to lose one eight-point game and be able to play again than to lose (in effect) two eight-point games; that's even more demoralizing. Accept the cube if you feel you have a proper basis for doing so; refuse it if you don't. But don't allow the number showing on the cube to influence your decision in any way. It's either a good take or a bad take; doubling it only makes it better or worse, not different.

In this regard, beware the allure of accepting a large double just because you are losing and are hopeful of winning it back in big chunks. This hope that springs eternal in every gambler's breast is really nothing but a tempting mirage. Almost invariably, you will wind up multiplying both your losings and your self-hatred for having been such a fool. For if the dice have been going against you, you *have* to bet cautiously until they change; if in fact your opponent is a better player, your playing for higher stakes will only increase your losses.

Of course, there are times when you feel that it's on the borderline of being a good take or not. Whenever I'm so undecided, I generally accept the cube. This is especially true when I'm winning, for as a famous gambler used to say, bet the sky when it's the other fellow's money, but play it close when it's your own. There's a certain validity to this, and so I tend to take these questionable doubles. My thinking is that since I have been winning thus far the combination of my luck and my strategy may continue. And should I in fact win such a game, my opponent will be even further demoralized. But even so, I do not take an obviously bad double. The principle remains the same, and should really be our third rule: accept the cube *only* if you feel you have a legitimate basis for doing so; have the courage to refuse it when you recognize realistically you have an inferior game.

There are other reasons which you should consider for accepting the cube in a borderline situation. First, there is the matter of odds, which I discussed earlier: a 3-to-1 gamble is not bad when your opponent is not that strong. Second, the cube is then in your possession. And, if in this instance it isn't a clear-cut case to refuse the double, it isn't too likely that you will be gammoned. However, there is now the assurance that you can play the game out to the end, with the possibility that right will overcome all adversity and you may yet gain the advantage. Should this happen, it obviously is of great value for you to have control of the pressure the cube can bring to bear.

In this regard, it is wise to keep the cube where it can be easily seen, so that you remain aware of it. I always keep it on the bar in front of me, rather than off to the side. Although there is an awkwardness to this—from time to time it gets knocked off, and has to be replaced—this positioning is crucial to keeping it constantly in mind. I have seen people so engrossed in their game that they completely forget the cube—and the right moment to throw it, like luck or love, is often fleeting. Keep it where you will see it; constantly be aware of it. That's rule number four.

Let's get into the use of the cube when there is no longer any contact. Here the situation is one of a mere race, and the use of the cube when you are somewhat ahead is to force out your opponent, in order to avoid the possible fickleness of the dice. In this situation, your conduct depends to a great extent on the courage and behavior pattern of your opponent in accepting the cube. If he generally accepts it, then you want to wait until you are fairly sure of the game. If he generally refuses it, you can throw it sooner. In the latter case, the question I would ask is why you have waited this long to throw it; you probably should have done so much earlier. In making the decision to throw (or accept) the cube, no consideration need be given to the matter of gammons, since it is evident that both players will be able to avoid that danger if they play out such a no-contact game.

Let's look at this situation:

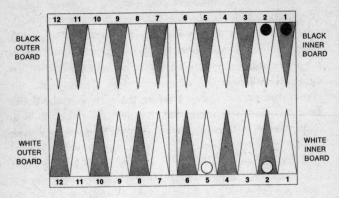

DIAGRAM 77

It is your throw, and you have men on your 2 and 5 points. (Remember our magic number from the last chapter?) Your opponent, with men on his 1 and 2 points, will get off on his next throw, as there is nothing he can roll that will not allow him to take both men off. Should you double? Yes, say I: if he accepts, you have more than an even chance to win double the bet. If he doesn't accept it, great: you have your money. So, when I have this board, or a better one, I always throw the cube.

If my opponent has a 2 and 5 position and throws the cube at me, do I take? Well, I do if it is exactly a 2 and 5 position that he has, and also if my position is at least a 2 and 5 as well. The reason is this: although he has better than a 50-50 chance of winning, there is still the factor of 3 to 1 odds working for me. So, although there are nineteen ways out of thirty-six for me to lose one dollar, there are seventeen ways out of thirty-six for me to stay alive and then have at least a 50-50 chance to win three. Therefore, the odds paradoxically are with me to accept.

If he is even one point better for either of his men, I generally don't take the double. Why? Because with either a 1 and 5 position or a 2 and 4 position he has twenty-three out of thirty-six ways of getting off. Here, it's not worth my taking the chance, and so I refuse the cube, pay the dollar and hate him even more! So, rule five: remember 2 - 5 to throw the cube; accept it with your 2 - 5 unless he's even one point better.

Now, since the dice have no memory and there is no reason to expect your second throw to have other probabilities than the first, the same rule holds true when you each have four men left on the board. Indeed, it is even more fun to watch your opponent squirm when he has three men left to your four! You can lose some heartbreakers, as when he gets a double, but the excitement and the probabilities both make it worth your while—if you don't already have an ulcer to contend with.

In bearing off, and with a proper distribution of men, the probability is that eight throws (sixteen dice) are all that is necessary. (Remember, I am talking about a no-contact situation.) Although doubles should occur one and one-third times out of eight throws, since doubles can occur equally for either of you I will disregard them here. And because I desire simplicity and efficiency, I don't bother counting specifically these necessary eight throws. What I do count is any inequitable distribution of men in terms of additional throws that consequently may be necessary.

If as I suggested we disregard doubles, then in thirty throws—that is, with sixty dice—the probability is that each number will show ten times, or one out of six. So, for every six throws—twelve dice—the probability is that each number should show twice. Therefore, I consider it an equitable distribution when I have twelve of my men spread two to a point on the six points, and with no more than one of the other three men on the upper half of my inner board (that is, on the 4, 5, or 6 points). This is because I should throw a 1, 2, or 3 as often as a 4, 5, or 6, and so if more than one man (of these three) is on the upper half of the inner board I cannot count on getting him off in the allotted number of throws. Therefore, for each extra man on points above the 3, I count an additional half throw (one die). I also count an additional half throw for any point that is blank, if there is a higher point that has men on it, for this very often necessitates moving a man within the board.

For me, this is the important count—how many additional half throws are necessary for me to bear off, as contrasted to how many my opponent needs. We might call this comparison shopping. I am judging my inner board versus his, and quickly estimating the cost—in terms of the additional number of throws—necessary for each of us to get off. And this evaluation is what determines how I use the cube. Take the board in Diagram 78 on page 149, for example.

I would quickly evaluate this as my being two throws better than Black, and so I would throw the cube at him. I figure it thus: on the lower half of my inner board—the 1, 2, and 3 points—I have four men more than he. But this isn't as important as the upper half—the 4, 5, and 6 points. Here I have at least a one-throw advantage as far as the 4 point is concerned, we are equal on the 5, and I have a half throw advantage on the 6 point. This, combined with the strength I show on the 1 and 2 points, would prompt me to throw the cube, especially when I take into consideration the fact that

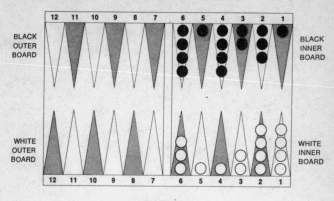

BLACK
OUTER
BOARD

BLACK
INNER
BOARD

WHITE
OUTER
BOARD

WHITE
INNER
BOARD

DIAGRAM 78

I have the dice (otherwise I could not offer the cube) and so, after my throw, I should be three throws ahead! If he takes it, he's a fool; I wouldn't take it if the positions were reversed. My rule here is that I double when I'm two throws ahead.

What to do when I have a closed board—a prime—and he has a man on the bar? Let's say I have taken off two of my men, with thirteen left to bear off, and the board looks like Diagram 79 on page 150.

Should I double? Well, let's count it out. I need a minimum of seven throws (again not counting on doubles) to bear off. It may even require eight throws, if I have to make a "safe" move to avoid being hit. As for Black, he will probably require two throws to get in and two more to get this man around to his inner board. He probably will also be able to get both his men on the B11 and B8 points in on one throw. Therefore, the probabilities are that Black will be able to start bearing off on his sixth throw. Consequently,

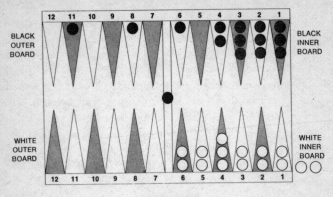

DIAGRAM 79

the chances of my getting him on a gammon are not good; against this slight possibility is the larger danger of my having to leave a blot and his hitting it, which could suddenly turn the tables completely. So, in this case, I would throw the cube and hope he refuses it.

Let's change the board a bit:

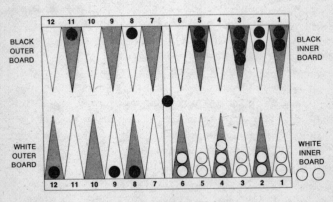

DIAGRAM 80

Here, Black still needs four throws to get his man on the bar into his inner board. But the men on W8 and W9 probably need one and a half throws each, the men on W12 and B11 need one throw each, and the man on B8 needs half a throw. This means a probable total of nine and a half throws before Black can begin bearing off. Therefore, because there is a good chance of a gammon, and because his back game position is virtually non-existent, I would not double.

Let's get to counting from the outer board. Here, the comparison shopping is generally based on the relative number of throws we each need to get into our inner boards and begin bearing off. Obviously, if most of the men being counted are out of the inner board, then the relative positions in it are of little moment. But if the game is fairly advanced, and there are relatively few men outside the inner board, the comparison of the inner boards must be taken into account as well.

My decision to throw the cube is based on a simple formula: for every eight throws necessary to win, I want to have at least a two-throw advantage (before my next throw) in order to offer the cube. By this I mean that if I need six throws to get all my men into my inner board, I will not offer the cube unless my opponent seems to need at least eight. And as the number of throws required gets larger, because the game is not that advanced, I wait until my edge gets greater or the game has substantially progressed, since two or three lucky (or unlucky) throws can too easily upset this small advantage. This is especially so against the sophisticated player I mentioned who knows the odds, for he—as I—would generally accept a double in such a situation. I will accept the cube even with a disadvantage of three moves out of eight if it is early in the game. Later, I generally play it by feel.

Anyway, this method of counting works. As you get used to it, you can do comparison shopping quickly. And this information, together with your judgment of your opponent's pattern of behavior, should quickly make back for you the price of this book.

There are several other points I'd like to make about doubling.

When I throw the cube, as with all of my play, I try to demonstrate a confidence in my act that admits of no self-doubt whatsoever. I make it very plain to my opponent that I know what I'm doing, and that if he takes my double he is at best a fool. And I do the same when I accept a double. Now, this may be only a small edge, and obviously there is no way to measure just how much this rattles an opponent, but I have no question about its overall value, and I recommend it to you.

In this respect you should know about beavers. A beaver is rarely used, but if you do use it—and pull it off—you can be sure your opponent will hesitate measurably before throwing the cube at you again. A beaver is a double double, and works like this: if your opponent throws the cube at you, and you know he has made a grievous error in doing so, you have the right—if you wish—not only to accept it, but *immediately* (that is, before he throws) to re-double the stakes. The gimmick is that you retain control of the cube as well! So, assume he throws the cube at you for two; before he throws you not only accept it but turn it to four! In theory he should be perfectly willing to accept it, since he expected —and was willing to chance—winning two. If he doesn't take the beaver, he has to pay you the two, for you in effect accepted that double before re-doubling. Of course, he will probably take it, but his jaw may hang a little loose. Your attitude, should you lose such a game, is that you almost made it; if you do win it, you've really got your friend demoralized for life—and you can now use the cube almost with abandon.

As for re-doubling, some players suggest that there are times when it is wise to double, but not re-double. This is nonsense. If the time is ripe to double it makes no difference whether the cube is at a 2, 4, 8, or whatever. A double is worthwhile or not worthwhile based only on the status of the game at that moment and the probabilities involved; it is not dependent on where the cube is or how much higher it will go. If it is not worth doubling to 16, it is not worth doing for 2.

Some players suggest that automatic doubles be limited to one or two; the implication is that only hustlers allow unlimited doubles. I don't agree with this, either. (Automatic doubles, in case you've forgotten, occur when both dice come up the same when you're each throwing one die to determine who has the first move; the cube is moved up one notch.) There is no rule on this; some players do not allow such doubles, others limit them, as I said. But I think that if the dice keep coming up doubles, well, so be it: I keep turning the cube. There is no hustling involved: each man has controlled one die. And so I play the doubles the way the dice dictate. It really helps stimulate the adrenalin, which is what the game is all about anyway.

You should also know about settlements. Some players accept settlements; I have never played this way and don't care to. In effect, it goes something like this: one player says to the other, "The cube is at eight and I'm going to throw it at you for sixteen; since you're crazy enough to accept it, and since no one knows what might happen with the dice, I'll take six now and let it go at that." His opponent: "Four." So maybe they settle for five. They sound like used car salesmen.

There really is no way to evaluate a settlement, and so there are no guidelines; it's simply a matter of haggling over terms. I have seen people offer settlements when I felt they had an excellent chance of winning, and I was astounded at their insecurity. For that's what it really is: insecurity on both sides. Neither one feels he is strong enough to win, and so in effect they both give up. If either believed in his position, he wouldn't settle. And so the only tip I can give you is if you are confident of your position, don't settle. But if you feel insecure about the dice, take the money and run when a settlement is offered to you.

But for me, settlements diminish the fun and excitement of the game; it's almost like a tourist suggesting he'll go only part way up in the Empire State Building if they'll reduce the price. Therefore, I don't play with settlements and I don't recommend them.

Now, for ease, here's a re-cap of the rules:

(1) Don't double too early.
(2) When you are further advanced than your opponent, and he no longer has a chance for a good back game, double.
(3) Have the courage to refuse the cube.
(4) Keep the cube where you will see it and constantly be aware of it.
(5) When bearing off, remember 2-5 to throw the cube; accept it with your 2-5 unless he's even one point better.
(6) Have at least a 1 in 4 advantage in throws before doubling.

And so, if you understand these few rules, you too can play diabolically—and for blood.

10. THE (SHORT) HISTORY OF BACKGAMMON

I once met someone who was an anthropologist or an archae-ologist, or something. He knew all about backgammon: its origins, its history. But I found him insufferably dull; he couldn't play.

However, here are his answers to the two most-asked questions about backgammon, questions which are always raised by those people just learning the game. (Once they have learned it, they're too busy playing to ask any others.)

Ur of the Chaldees, a name so poetically bizarre I will remember it forever, is where the earliest backgammon board has been found. It is no longer called Ur of the Chaldees; it is now part of what is called Iraq. And the board, which is no longer in Iraq but in the British Museum, has been dated by those who know at about 3,000 B.C. This impresses me; next to sex it is the oldest game in our civilization.

The second question people ask is about the doubling cube; my learned friend cannot help on this, nor can anyone else. The best knowledge about it is that it is an American invention, having been introduced by some anonymous genius in the early 1920s. Who he was, and how it began, no one really knows. Nor has the cube traveled: no other country uses it; it is strictly an American weapon.

Backgammon has been played throughout the world and throughout history; even without the cube it was considered to be the most exciting of gambling games. It was played by the Egyptians (a board was found in King Tut's tomb); by the Greeks (it is talked about by Plato, Sophocles, and Homer); by the Romans (Emperor Claudius presumably wrote a book on backgammon, but I haven't seen it); and I read somewhere that Antony played backgammon with Cleopatra. Among other things.

In France, today, it's called *tric-trac*, in Ireland *ticktack*. (How wonderfully phonetic, when you play—as they do—on wooden boards.) The Italians call it *Tavola Reale* and the Spanish *Tablas Reales:* both mean "royal tables." The mid-Easterners call it *tavloo,* for "doors." Variations of it are played everywhere: Russia, South America, Iceland, you name it.

It was always a big game with the English, having come to them via the Romans when Britain was invaded; the Latin *tabula* became the English *tables.* Chaucer referred to it in *The Canterbury Tales* ("They dancen and they play at ches and tables. . . ."); the Saxons were responsible for the name change (*baec* plus *gamen*), which began to be used in the seventeenth century.

And thence to us. Thomas Jefferson was a loser; river-boat gamblers (who used beautifully primitive wooden boards) were not. It is rumored that backgammon is part of the curriculum at our war colleges; all my attempts to obtain information on this (top secret?) matter have produced no positive results, but have doubtless led to a security check.

The game had its ups and downs in popularity in this country, never really becoming big until the 1920s when, as I said, the doubling cube was invented. Backgammon was just beginning to take on great popularity when the crash of '29 arrived to relegate it immediately to those few fortunates who still played in private clubs. And there it remained—until recently.

Which brings us to the question I'm curious about: whence the present—and enormous—resurgence of the game? (I know *why*; it's more fun than practically anything.) I'll light incense to the gods of *gamen* for anyone providing the answer. In the meantime—backgammon, anyone?

11. CHOUETTE

Chouette—pronounced "shoe-et"—is very much like the children's game of "king of the mountain," which is every man against the king until the king is deposed, and then it's every man, including the deposed king, against the new king. Yet one of the writers on backgammon calls chouette ". . . a more social form of the game."

I disagree.

I think that if you are playing for money, chouette is unquestionably an un-social form of the game and personally I hate it. The aggressive instincts one has toward a single opponent are enlarged to include many—and that is certainly anti-social. Furthermore, I find the lack of concentration (which is the trademark of chouette) to be a dissipation of energy; this is frustrating, nerve-wracking, and a bore.

Chouette is a dilettante's backgammon; it allows you to play at playing. It is a poor man's backgammon as well, since its only advantage is that several people can participate when there is only one board with which to play. However, since it is somewhat popular, I feel compelled to describe it.

In chouette, there is one man called "the man in the box" (the king of the mountain, as it were); he plays against all the other players, who are led by the "captain." Theoretically, there is no limit to the number of players; it simply requires a minimum of three. However, when you have more than five players participating, it gets both unwieldy and oppressively slow for the man at the bottom of the line.

At the outset, the order of play is determined by each of the players casting one die, with the player who rolls the highest number becoming the man in the box. The one with the next highest throw becomes the captain, and the rest of the players follow downward on the team in sequence, depending on their throw. If two or more men have thrown the same number, they throw again for their own relative positions, but behind anyone with a higher initial throw and ahead of anyone who had a lesser throw in the initial toss.

The man in the box plays against the captain, who is really the captain of a team of kibitzers. All of these team men are allowed to consult with the captain about moves. In practice they don't really do that much consultation, but they do a lot of moaning and groaning. This is one disadvantage of chouette, as far as I'm concerned: the noise. A second disadvantage is the time wasted, even if only once in a while, when the players consult. This becomes especially annoying if the captain is not that good a player and he continually needs advice from the other men on his team. A third annoyance is that the captain has the final say as to what the move will be, and this can be even more frustrating to a better player who may be inclined and able to take a risk, or who is better versed in the strategy of the game than the captain. There are times when you get a very stubborn player as the captain, and his obstinacy makes you want to punch him in the nose.

None of this sounds very social to me.

When you have a number of very good players who are playing chouette, the game can move a lot faster, but in such a case I see no value in playing a chouette as opposed to several head-to-head games concurrently. That's why I think chouette players are dilettantes. They wander, they chat with friends at the bar or at other tables—possibly this is what the other author meant when he said chouette is a more social form of the game.

The game proceeds this way: the man in the box plays against the team collectively, with the captain both leading the team and actually playing the game. If the team loses, each member must individually pay the man in the box the amount of the bet; that is, if the basic bet was a dollar, and there are six men on the team, then the man in the box wins six dollars—multiplied, of course, by the cube if it is used and by gammons if they occur. The captain, now disgraced, drops down to the last position on the team, and the man who had previously been next highest in rank to him becomes captain.

If the man in the box loses, he must pay the stakes to each of the members of the team, and he now joins the team as its lowest ranking member. The man who was captain becomes the man in the box, and the next ranking player to him becomes captain. And so it goes.

Gammons and backgammons are, of course, counted for full value when they occur.

The doubling cube works this way. If the man in the box doubles, each player on the team may accept or refuse the double, as he wishes. If he refuses it, he pays the man in the box the amount of the bet, and then remains out of the balance of that game; however, he does not lose his place in line. If the captain refuses the cube, though, and another man (or men) on the team wishes to accept it, then the highest-ranking man of those who accept it becomes captain for the rest of the game, and the man who was captain goes to the bottom of the line. Then, as this game plays out, should the man who accepted the double lose, he retains his original position in the line. Any man who was ahead of him, except the captain, still remains ahead of him, even if he had refused the cube, and the highest-ranking man now becomes the new captain. But should the man who accepted the double win, he now becomes the man in the box, with the deposed king going to the foot of the line (behind the ex-captain, who beat him there only by moments). And the highest-ranking player left, even if he had refused the cube, now becomes the captain.

The reverse situation works this way. If the captain wants to double, the team must go along with him. Usually, they are perfectly willing to do so, for the multiple increase in stakes puts enormous pressure on the man in the box, and especially if the team is large. A bet that's worth two dollars to each member of the team becomes ten or twelve for the man in the box if there are five or six players, and of course a gammon doubles everything. In some instances, however, a team member may not wish to go along with the double, and some players allow this man to drop out by having the captain buy his share. For example, should the captain wish to double, he pays the player who is not willing to go along with this a dollar for his share, and then the captain has two shares playing against the man in the box. This means, of course, that the captain either pays or collects on both.

Some players allow the man in the box to preempt the captain in paying off the player who does not want to go along with the captain's double; this is supposed to relieve some of the pressure that can be put on the box. And sometimes, when the team against him is large, the man in the box is allowed to take a partner; this too is done to relieve the pressure on him.

I find this somewhat silly. If you're playing a chouette, presumably you want the excitement of the added pressure that playing in the box gives you; consciously lessening this excitement defeats the main advantage of chouette. Also, when you start enlarging the game to the point that even the box needs a partner, you have also reached the point where you need to put numbers on players and keep a scorecard in order to tell who is which and where. You might even need a pair of fieldglasses to see the action.

There is a small value to chouette, however, if you are a beginner: it's a good way to hear differing points of view on various moves and strategies. I suggest you just keep your ears open and your mouth shut. Try to remember the points at issue so that you can reread the relevant sections in this book. Then evaluate it all; you'll be a much better player if you think it through for yourself.

But while at the chouette table, and still trying to learn, save yourself some aggravation and money by being a good follower. Not of the herd, but of whoever you think is the best player on the team. Parrot his lead; you might even make some money. And when you're in the box, where it can be costly, be very careful with the cube. Don't throw it; don't get nervous or upset when it's thrown at you. Again, the attitude of the various team players—especially the key man you've been following—may give you a clue as to how strong a position all of them think they have. If their attitude suggests invincibility and you're not too sure of yourself, don't accept the cube.

But if and when you do accept the cube, hold on to it. Don't re-double. You may be tempted to at some point, thinking you're strong enough, and also being anxious to establish yourself as one of the big men, but beware: you are still backgammon young and in need of gentle nurturing. If you were right in wanting to re-double, and in fact had a strong enough position to have done so, there still is no embarrassment in merely winning a doubled game. If you were wrong in wanting to re-double, then you've just been saved the egg on the face. So, until you have a decent sense of what you're doing, don't touch the cube except (possibly) to accept it, and then only if you are sure!

You also can do something to avoid the box, if you're afraid of it. Simply refuse the double if it is thrown at you when you are highest in succession, especially when you are captain. This will keep returning you to the bottom of the line, and unless you get unlucky and win when you're captain you need never play in the box.

Finally, learner or not: if you're going to play chouette, two small words of caution. First, don't advise often; the less you talk, the more attention will be paid to you when you do. Save your comments for moments when you feel strongly; don't waste them on moves that can legitimately be made either way. Second, when you are captain, listen to and genuinely evaluate the advice given you. Play your own game, but be open and flexible enough to realize that there are other good players at the table, and one of them might be an even bigger genius than you.

12. TOURNAMENT SURVIVAL

In the first chapter of this book I spoke of the casino operators: those gamblers who don't gamble, yet are the only consistent winners at the gaming tables. So it is only fitting that I come full circle in this closing chapter and talk about the only consistent winners at backgammon: the tournament operators. They don't play, they don't bet, they just organize. But they keep collecting.

Occasionally a charity serves as bait; it gets some piece of the action. But the organizers of the event are the big winners.

Now, I have nothing against a guy making an honest buck for putting together an entertainment if it's well done, but I really object to the quasi social club goulash that most of these tournaments are. I don't think an organizer should get a bundle merely because he has a good mailing list or better press agent; I think he also has an obligation to his customers to make it all work smoothly and enjoyably.

I cannot stand starting hours later than advertised, so that you end what should be an evening's fun well into the next day, when it's no longer fun; I abhor mediocre food, which is what is generally served at extortion prices; and I resent the usual lack of organization that results in everyone's being treated—and behaving—like a herd of leaderless cattle. And since I work hard for my money, I prefer the zero-sum game: that is, one in which the winnings and losings are paid directly between the two players involved, and no third party—organizer or casino—gets a piece.

However, since some people do like tournaments and enter them frequently, here are a few thoughts on the subject.

First, if you are in a tournament such as I've described, complain. Not to the organizer, for he's only there on a one-night stand and is probably the prime cause of your discomfort. Complain to the manager of the restaurant or club where the tournament is being held; since his name is being misused he has a vested interest in at least trying to avoid a repeat performance. And if the message begins to get around that the paying guests expect a little respect for their sanity and stomachs, changes may occur. Tournaments can be run smoothly and well; for the money they charge they should be.

Read the rule sheets that are passed out; if you don't get one (I've rarely seen a tournament with enough for everyone) borrow someone's. Know in particular the number of points needed in each round to win, and also check the rules concerning the doubling cube. In general, tournaments allow the cube to be used in all levels of play except beginners. However, the strategy in using the cube in tournaments varies somewhat from normal play.

Since the winner of each round is usually determined by the achievement of a fixed number of points rather than winning a certain number of games, and there is no difference in winning a round by a large number of points or merely by one, you should constantly be aware of the number of points still necessary to win the round in order to decide on the proper use of the cube. For example, if you're playing an eleven-point match and you're leading ten points to nine, you obviously will win the round if you simply win the game, and so to double will be of no value to you. You won't force your opponent out, no matter how bad his position; the cube is consequently of no value to you at this moment.

However, if you should be the one behind, and your opponent needs but one point to win the match, you should always throw the cube at him. If the score against you is ten to nine, this means you can win the match if you win the game, as opposed to merely tieing it if you don't throw the cube. If you lose the game, then you've lost the round no matter where the cube is. And if you are even further behind in the score, you are playing catch-up and need every point you can get; therefore, throw the cube. Also, throw it instantly the game begins—that is, on your very first roll of the dice. Since you have no alternative but to throw it, why not do so immediately and put instant pressure on your opponent?

The same principle is true should your opponent need two points to win and throw the cube at you. You may refuse it, because your position is poor and you still have at least one more chance, or you may feel that your opponent has made a mistake in offering the cube and you therefore accept it. However, if you do play it out, don't just accept the cube if you need more than two points to win the match: in this case, *beaver* him! And should you need more than four points to win (which is what the game is now worth), then immediately afterward—on your next roll—throw the cube right back at him! You will achieve not only total consternation, but also the enviable alternatives of a game worth eight points should he accept the cube, or four points added to your score if he doesn't. For you, it was very simple: if you accepted the cube in the first place, then he will win the match if he wins the game; you therefore have nothing to lose by making the stakes as high as possible—and maybe everything to gain.

Because of this situation, where a losing player can at some point use the cube with abandon, and possibly thereby affect the outcome of the match in what some think to be an unfair manner, limitations on the use of the doubling cube have been suggested. Only one is commonly used today; it is called the Crawford rule. It provides that in any match, when one player has arrived at a position of needing only one point more to win, the doubling cube may not be used in the next game, but may be used freely thereafter. That is, for the one game immediately after the leading player has reached a score of one point less than he needs to win the round, the doubling cube may not be used at all. But then, if the match is not settled after this short moratorium, the cube may again be used without restraint. This provision therefore offers the player who is on the brink of victory a one game safety against the double. And it behooves you to know whether this rule is in effect, and to play accordingly.

Always be wary of gammons and backgammons; know what they—in conjunction with the cube—can do to the score. At times it may be wiser to forgo continuing a back game attempt for as long as you might under other circumstances.

If the seating is not pre-arranged, try to get off in a corner somewhere, away from the terminal-like traffic near the tables of the scorekeepers. That area will be bedlam, and the further you are from it the better.

If you should win in any round, don't stand there waiting for congratulations. Get to the chart where the players are listed and check on the match whose winner you will play next. If they are still playing, go over to their table and watch them. You can get some idea of the strategy and tactics used by each of them. Hopefully this "scouting" will be of some advantage when you play the winner.

Play at your own pace. In tournaments, even more than in head-to-head play, there is a tendency to rush. Avoid it. Rushing leads to mistakes; we know where *they* lead. Although technically the judges may impose a time limit on play, I've never seen it done even under the most excruciating of circumstances. Besides, if they are going to do it, they will warn you first.

A spectator may be annoying you, for a logical or even an illogical reason. Generally, you have the right under most tournaments' rules to ask a judge to remove that person. If the rules of the particular tournament don't provide for this, insist on it anyway. You paid your entry and you're entitled to it. Besides, doing so may even rattle your opponent, which is a nice bonus. But more important, it keeps you from being rattled.

Finally, if the tournament is at a club you don't know, and therefore the food is a question mark, eat before you go. Or carry a candy bar. It may turn out to be your salvation.

APPENDIX: THE RULES OF BACKGAMMON AND THEIR VARIANTS IN PLAY

These are the rules of backgammon, which were promulgated in 1931 by the Backgammon and Cards Committee of the Racquet and Tennis Club of New York. They have been adopted as official by just about everyone and every club that's given any thought to the matter. Some of these rules are not practiced today, for one reason or another; I'll point them out at the end. Here they are.

THE GAME

(1) The game of backgammon is played by two persons.

(2) Thirty men—fifteen of one color and fifteen of

another—are used, and are set up as shown below, on a standard board, of four quarters or tables having six points each.

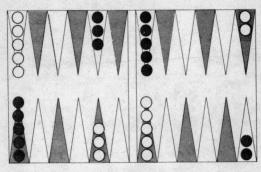

DIAGRAM 81

(3) For entering and throwing off, the points in both inner tables are considered as numbered from 1 to 6, beginning with the point nearest the light.

(4) Direction of play is from adversary's inner table to adversary's outer table, to player's outer table, and then to player's inner (home) table.

(5) Play of the men is governed by two dice, thrown (cast) from a cup in which the dice are shaken before casting.

(6) Choice of seats, men, set-up, dice, etc., shall be made by the player winning the opening throw

THE THROWS

(7) For the opening throw each player throws a single die. Every tie requires another opening throw. Whoever

throws the higher number wins, and for his first move plays the numbers upon both dice. After that each player in turn throws two dice.

(8) The dice must be rolled together and come to rest flat (not "cocked") upon the tables at the player's right, otherwise they must be thrown again.

(9) If a throw is made before an adversary's play is completed, or if either player touches a die before it has come to rest, the adversary of the offender may require a rethrow.

(10) The player must leave his dice upon the board until his play is completed. Should he pick them up or turn them over before the completion of his play, the adversary may declare the play void and require the offender to replace the man or men moved and to throw again.

THE PLAY

(11) The play of the men consists:

(a) In moving a man the exact number of points indicated by the number on a die thrown.

(b) Entering a man, in the adversary's inner table, on a point corresponding to the number on a die thrown.

(c) Throwing off (bearing) a man in player's inner table—when no man is left outside that table or on the bar—from a point corresponding to the number on a die thrown, or as provided in Law 15.

Doublets require four plays—if possible—of the die number thrown.

(12) No play may be made which lands on a point held by two or more of the adversary's men.

(13) When a play lands on a single man (blot) of

the adversary's, such man is "hit," and must be lifted and placed on the bar for entry in the player's inner table.

(14) A player having a man on the bar may not play until that man has been entered.

(15) Plays must be made for both dice if possible. Either number may be played first. If only one number can be played, and there is a choice, the higher must be played.

In throwing off, a man may at all times be correctly thrown off from the highest occupied point which is lower than the number indicated by a die. If a number is thrown for an unoccupied point, no man below can be thrown off, for such number, while any man remains on a higher point.

(16) Whenever a man has been moved correctly and quitted (the player's hand removed), that play cannot be changed.

ERRORS

(17) If an error has been made in the set-up, either player may correct it prior to the completion of his first play.

(18) If an error in play has been made, either player may require its correction before a subsequent throw, but not thereafter. The man played in error must be correctly played if possible.

SCORING

(19) A game is won by the player who first throws (bears) off all of his men.

A gammon (double game) is won if the adversary has not thrown off a single man. This doubles the count for a single game.

A backgammon (triple game) is won if the adversary

has not thrown off a single man, and has one or more men in the winner's inner table or upon the bar. This triples the count for a single game.

(20) The count is raised: Automatically—

By agreement, each tie of the opening throw may either:

(a) Double the previous count.

(b) Add one to the previous count.

Unless an understanding has been reached as to the method and limitation of automatic raises they are not played.

Voluntarily—

Either player may offer the first optional double of the previous count. After that the right to double the previous count alternates, being always with the player who has accepted the last double.

In every case, a double may be offered only when it is the player's turn to play and before he has thrown the dice. A double may be accepted or declined. The refusal of a double terminates the game, and the player refusing loses whatever his count may amount to at that time. Gammons and backgammons double or triple the last count.

(21) By agreement, other methods of scoring may be used, such as:

The Point Game. In this 1 point is scored, by the winner of a game, for each man left in the adversary's inner table; 2 points are scored for each man left in the adversary's outer table; 3 points for each man left in the winner's outer table, and 4 points for each man left in the winner's inner table or upon the bar.

Here are some of today's variations on the rules; where options exist it is wise to discuss them with your opponent before starting to play so that no questions arise during the game.

Rule 6. The dice are usually picked at random, but at the beginning of any game a player can ask that they be re-chosen. In this event he shakes the four dice in one cup and throws them out; his opponent then picks one, he takes one, his opponent takes his second die, and the player takes the last.

Rule 7. Some players allow the man who throws the higher die to refuse this move and instead to re-cast both dice to determine his first move; in this case they sometimes also move the doubling cube up one notch, although leaving it in the center of the bar, where it is initially available to either. In this event, the player must take the second roll, even if it is not as good as the one he refused.

If they use this option, many players then also allow the second man to refuse *his* roll if he doesn't like it, but only if the cube is again turned up one notch.

I like to play with only the first half of this option: that is, the player who has the higher die but isn't too happy with this move may re-cast both dice and then use this roll for his move; the cube does get turned up once. There are two reasons for this: first, purely emotionally, I want to be the one throwing the two dice that control my move. (My emotions are easily overcome, however, if that first bipartisan throw happens to be a good one.) Second, this allows the first player the chance of an opening double, which he is denied if you play according to the original rule; I think having this possibility adds excitement and fairness to the game. I say "fairness," for doubles are valuable and I don't think the opening player who has won the right of the first move should be denied this important weapon. And since the second player is not denied this possibility, I see no reason why he should have the option of a re-roll, thereby doubling his chances of hitting a blot the first player may leave. This gives him an inordinate advantage, and I don't like it.

Rule 10. This rule really has no meaning today in view of the common practice of handling the dice, which I describe below in my comment on Rule 16.

Rule 15. The description in this rule of bearing off leaves much to be desired; the committee preparing the rules suffered a remarkable relapse on this one. If you have any questions about bearing off read through the pertinent section in Chapter Two.

Rule 16. Most players I know do not follow this rule; they allow the move to be changed, even several times. The player signifies that his move is completed by picking up his dice; *then* the play cannot be changed (if it is correct). If the player should pick up his dice before completing his move, then his opponent has the right to compel the balance of the move or not as he wishes. And the roll by the opponent automatically accepts the move; thereafter it cannot be changed. (I've written about incorrect moves in Chapter Two, which might be worthwhile consulting again.)

Rule 19. Some players do not allow backgammons, although they do count gammons. Why, I'm not sure, unless they simply can't face the ignominy of a triple defeat. But it seems to me that the possibility of a backgammon makes the strategy of playing a back game that much more exciting, and so I like them and recommend them.

There are also some players who do not allow gammons in games that have not been *voluntarily* doubled at least once; the theory is that this loosens up a possibly dullish game by allowing the player who is behind to become a little flagrant in his moves in an attempt to shock his opponent into a state of confusion. Should the cube be thrown, he can refuse it; until then he can play with abandon. In practice, however, all it does is coddle the lesser player; I don't think he should stay out late at night playing backgammon if he needs this kind of protection.

Rule 20. In the initial casting of the dice for the first move, when each player throws one die, a tie may be thrown. In this event many players turn the cube up one notch each time this happens. Some players limit this practice, so that the cube may be turned up the once, but not again, no matter how many times ties are thrown. And, of course, some cowards don't allow turning the cube at all. Here, you take your choice.

Finally, since someone is always coming up with his own hustle, I suggest you stay away from any other proposed variants that are not covered here. Stick with the old faithfuls. They've worked for a good long time. And by the looks of things, they'll be working for a long time to come.

The one essential guidebook for anyone
who has ever had trouble saying
"NO."

CREATIVE AGGRESSION

The Art of Assertive Living

Are you letting "nice guys" ruin your life? Or are you
just being "nice" and ruining your own? Now Dr.
George R. Bach, author of the smash bestsellers
THE INTIMATE ENEMY and **PAIRING**, shows
the terrible price of "nice"—the illness, depression,
and hidden hostility that can wreck a "nice guy's" life
—plus sound, workable ways to express your natural
anger constructively. Find an exhilarating new free-
dom in your everyday life—through **CREATIVE
AGGRESSION!**

Selected by **THE LITERARY GUILD** and
PSYCHOLOGY TODAY Book Clubs

38042/$2.25

Where better paperbacks are sold, or directly from
the publisher. Include 25¢ per copy for mailing;
allow 4-6 weeks for delivery. Avon Books, Mail
Order Dept., 250 West 55th Street, New York, N.Y.
10019.

CA 2-78

AVON   THE BEST IN
BESTSELLING ENTERTAINMENT

☐	**Shanna** Kathleen E. Woodiwiss	38588	$2.25
☐	**The Enchanted Land** Jude Devereux	40063	$2.25
☐	**Love Wild and Fair** Bertrice Small	40030	$2.50
☐	**Your Erroneous Zones**		
	Dr. Wayne W. Dyer	33373	$2.25
☐	**Tara's Song** Barbara Ferry Johnson	39123	$2.25
☐	**The Homestead Grays** James Wylie	38604	$1.95
☐	**Hollywood's Irish Rose** Nora Bernard	41061	$1.95
☐	**Baal** Robert R. McCammon	36319	$2.25
☐	**Dream Babies** James Fritzhand	35758	$2.25
☐	**Fauna** Denise Robins	37580	$2.25
☐	**Monty: A Biography of Montgomery Clift**		
	Robert LaGuardia	37143	$2.25
☐	**Majesty** Robert Lacey	36327	$2.25
☐	**Death Sails the Bay** John R. Feegel	38570	$1.95
☐	**Q & A** Edwin Torres	36590	$1.95
☐	**If the Reaper Ride** Elizabeth Norman	37135	$1.95
☐	**This Other Eden** Marilyn Harris	36301	$2.25
☐	**Emerald Fire** Julia Grice	38596	$2.25
☐	**Ambassador** Stephen Longstreet	31997	$1.95
☐	**Gypsy Lady** Shirlee Busbee	36145	$1.95
☐	**Good Evening Everybody**		
	Lowell Thomas	35105	$2.25
☐	**All My Sins Remembered** Joe Haldeman	39321	$1.95
☐	**The Search for Joseph Tully**		
	William H Hallahan	33712	$1.95
☐	**Moonstruck Madness** Laurie McBain	31385	$1.95
☐	**ALIVE: The Story of the Andes Survivors**		
	Piers Paul Read	39164	$2.25
☐	**Sweet Savage Love** Rosemary Rogers	38869	$2.25
☐	**The Flame and the Flower**		
	Kathleen E. Woodiwiss	35485	$2.25
☐	**I'm OK—You're OK**		
	Thomas A. Harris M.D.	28282	$2.25

Available at better bookstores everywhere, or order direct from the publisher.

AVON BOOKS, Mail Order Dept., 224 W. 57th St., New York, N.Y. 10019
Please send me the books checked above. I enclose $_____ (please include 50¢ per copy for postage and handling). Please use check or money order—sorry, no cash or C.O.D.'s. Allow 4-6 weeks for delivery.

Mr/Mrs/Miss _____

Address _____

City _____ State/Zip _____

BBBB 1-79

THE NATION'S #1 BESTSELLER

ONE FULL YEAR ON THE NEW YORK TIMES BESTSELLER LIST!

The one book that will make you realize the power inherent in your own life.

YOUR ERRONEOUS ZONES

DR. WAYNE W. DYER

Wayne Dyer is the supreme advertisement for his own product—a practicing therapist and counselor, he has followed his own advice to become a coast-to-coast celebrity, appearing on over 700 radio and television shows.

His message is simple and direct.

It can show you how to cut through a lifetime of emotional red tape once and for all. It can help you achieve firm control of who and what you are. And, very possibly, it can be the catalyst for great life-enhancing change!

SELECTED BY FOUR MAJOR BOOK CLUBS

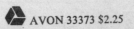 AVON 33373 $2.25   ERR 9-77